6-13·74

The European Community in the world

Proceedings of the Conference of the Institute for International Studies and the Europe Institute, University of Leyden, 'The external relations of the enlarged European Community', May 1971

The European Community in the world

The external relations of
the enlarged European Community

Edited by

Ph. P. Everts

*Director Institute for International
Studies, University of Leyden*

Rotterdam University Press/1972

ISBN: 90 237 2236 1

Contents

Introduction

In May 1971 the Institute for International Studies of the University of Leyden, together with the Europe Institute of the same university, organized a two-day conference under the title 'The enlarged European Community and its relations with the other European countries and the countries of the Third World'.

The papers presented and discussed at this conference are collected in this volume. Some of them were re-written and enlarged, in the light of the discussions, for the purpose of this publication. The main idea behind the organization of this conference was, that the likely enlargement of the European Community from six to nine or ten members would, as a matter of course, have a number of important political and economic consequences. But while much has been said and written about the problems directly connected with the entry of Great Britain and the other candidate-members into the European Community and about the impact this enlargement will have on the structure and functioning of the Community, much less has been written on the impact which this extension will have on the rest of the world. Although the political and economic effects will be felt in many areas of the world, two of these were singled out for discussion: 'The rest of Europe', including both the countries of the Socialist Bloc and the neutrals and the developing countries of the Third World. Two sets of questions were applied to both areas: what will be the effect of the enlargement of the European Economic Community on these countries and on its relations with them? Will the extension be favorable, neutral or detrimental to their development and to the development of cooperative, mutually favorable, relations? Is the EEC becoming a new imperialistic superpower or is it a necessary and healthy development, anticipating new worldwide structures?

The book, therefore, is divided into two parts with seemingly little connection between the two. But there is a link in the sense that the choices and options, facing 'Europe' (i.e. in this connection: Western Europe, thus reflecting a quite common bias) in both areas are similar in structure and conception. Two visions on the integration process prevail. On the one hand there is the vision of a continuous process of integration, deepening in scope and extending in domain, ending up finally in a federal union with a common foreign and military policy.

1

This process of integration is the primary goal, if need be, at the expense of others outside the Community.

The problems of the world in the political, economic, ecological and other fields can only be successfully dealt with if there are structures fit for doing so, and if there is a beginning of order. For there can be no justice without order. And as long as worldwide structures do not exist or are ineffective, one should start at a lower level. Only through unity can Europe hope to offer a counterweight to the other blocs or superpowers: the USA, Eastern Europe and the Soviet Union, Japan and China.

The adherents of the other option are not entirely convinced that only those things should be undertaken separately, which cannot be done collectively. Their vision of Europe is an open one. Ever increasing integration in Western Europe may make it more instead of less difficult to solve a number of problems. If the process of integration continues, one may well end up with a political bloc, which will no doubt want to have its own nuclear weapons. And this would be the end of the process of 'detente' with Eastern Europe. This vision also implies the conviction that the inwardlooking, protectionist aspects of the integration process are highly unfavorable for the development of the Third World, if one cannot speak of outright exploitation. Further integration should be made conditional upon the degree to which it does not prevent arrangements which are wider in scope and multilateral in a more real sense.

These seem to be the major trends. There are, of course, a number of other models and these can be refined and specified. A number of them are outlined in *Prof. Brugmans'* contribution to this volume. *John Pinder* deals with the question how a common policy, in the economic field, toward the Eastern European countries and the Soviet Union can and should be elaborated. He is more optimistic about the possibilities of a policy that stimulates developments in the East (and the West) which would be beneficial to both sides and yet would not be provocative, than are some others, like *Alfred Mozer*, who, in his discussion of the role and problems of some of the European neutrals, not only shows some scepticism about their possibility to play a role in bridging the gap between West and East, but also cautions against uncoordinated bilateralism and efforts to single out Eastern European countries, because of the dangers inherent in such politics.

Dr. J. Kaufmann, in his paper, discusses the possibilities of institutionalisation of East-West relations and deals in detail with the role and prospects of the United Nations Economic Commission for Europe and the model which it might offer to forms of cooperation.

In the second part two views are presented on the role of the European Economic Community with regard to the development of the countries of the Third World. Although both are critical of the performance of the EEC in this respect, *R. Cohen,* looking at the Community 'from the inside' is much more optimistic about the chances of a common policy which sincerely has the development of the developing countries as its aim. He stresses the need for and the inevitability of such a policy.

H. A. J. Coppens, on the other hand, rejects this common policy, on the basis of this analysis of the past record of the Community. Such a policy would continue to strengthen the hierarchical international system, would in his opinion prevent multilateral arrangements and hinder those countries which are willing to follow more liberal and farreaching policies.

Finally *Prof. H. H. Maas* offers a summary of the debates and evaluates the symposium, in which he stresses a number of the questions which were not discussed or just touched upon and which merit further consideration.

A number of the questions and divergent views were vigorously discussed. These discussions are presented here in summary. The editor has tried to be faithful and objective in his reporting of the discussion, but acknowledges that some of his biases may have crept in through his editorial work, for which he apologizes. He is very greatful to all those who assisted in the preparation of the conference and this book. Special gratitude goes to all the authors, who have given so much of their time in preparing and re-writing their papers.

Leyden, December 1971

Philip P. Everts
director Institute for
International Studies

Contributors

H. Brugmans, Rector of the College of Europe, Bruges, Belgium

R. Cohen, Assistant Chief Executive of the Commission of the European Communities, Brussels, Belgium

H. A. J. Coppens, Research associate, Department of Economics, Free University of Amsterdam, Netherlands

Ph. P. Everts, Director of the Institute for International Studies, University of Leyden, Netherlands

J. Kaufmann, Ambassador of the Netherlands to the Organization for Economic Cooperation and Development, Paris, France

H. H. Maas, Professor in the Law of International Organizations and Director of the Europa Instituut, University of Leyden, Netherlands

A. Mozer, Formerly Chief Executive of the Commission of the European Communities, Epse, Netherlands

J. Pinder, Director of Political and Economic Planning, London, England

5

Part I

Errata

Page	Line	For	Reads
146	13	thereby reducing	thereby relatively reducing
147	39/40	perpetuating	maintaining
157	6	production	import
157	7	are capable of hampering trade	are hampering trade
157	7	import	production
157	16	colza	rape seed
157	16	suflowerseed	sunfloweroil
157	33	drawbacks	restitutions
159	14	'surprise'	'surpri'
160	4	in the investment projects	of the allocations
164	14	the fundamental decision	the decision in principle
164	34	Lastly	Further
164	41	reference to	starting with
165	17	rights	tariffs
173	33	regulated entirely	regulated almost entirely
174	31	realise	receive
174	40	to oblige their opposite numbers	to please their colleagnes
175	19/20	Beetgrowers	Beetgrower's Assocations
176	38	aid	cooperation
178	1/2	contradistinction	contradiction
179	12	criticises the American T.P. Thornton for writing	quotes the American T.P. Thornton:
179	23	(unpublished stencil, Vienna, aug. '70)	(unpublished stencil, Vienna, Aug. '70). Later published as: A structural theory of imperialism (in: Journal of Peace Research, no. 2, 1971).
179	26	concord	harmony
179	34	community	harmony
180	26	the payment balances	the balances of payment
180	27	from the strings attacted to the aid	from the tying of the aid
181	41	orders	regulations
183	12	award	payment

Twelve 'models' for European Union

H. BRUGMANS

I. Today, it is rather unusual to come across responsible writers or statesmen who would declare that they are against European union 'in principle'. This only ones who do so are to be found on the extreme Right and the extreme Left, among Fascists and Communists. Of course their motives are different, but this does not necessarily preclude – and in fact has not always precluded – action pursued in common or at least in parallel agreement.

In this respect, the traditional Fascists, such as can be found in certain sections of the Movimento Sociale Italiano, are hardly of interest. They indulge in nostalgic dreams of national grandeur, to be defended both against America and the Communists. However, anti-Communism may lead these circles to a reluctant acceptance of NATO and possibly even a kind of European co-operation.

At times, Right-wing Nationalism has sought geographic enlargement, leading to an authoritarian kind of Europeanism, for instance in a German movement which characteristically called itself 'Nation Europa'. A similar view is held by the Belgian 'collaborator' Jean Thiriart, whose book, *400 Millions d'Hommes – l'Europe, La Naissance d'Une Nation, au Départ d'un Parti historique* (published by the author in May 1964), is a hymn to European Centralism and Racialism.

On their part, the official Communist parties, in spite of their internationalist tradition, have constantly advocated national sovereignty as an essential part of their doctrine. Of course, this statement applies only to the West-European countries, where even the most outdated chauvinist arguments were used against any integration scheme: violently anti-German articles and cartoons appeared in the Paris *Humanité* during the battle around EDC: they speak volumes in that respect. By contrast, in the satellite states, the so-called Brezhnev-doctrine is applied, which means insistence on the 'limited sovereignty' of those countries already in the Soviet Realm.

For some time, however, it has seemed as if unconditional Communist opposition to West-European union is on the wane, especially in the Italian Party, whereas the Communist-led Confédération Général du Travail in France, is slowly following in that same direction. The presence of both CGT and the Italian Confederazione Generale Italiano del Lavoro in the Consultative Social and Economic Committee of the European Commission, as well as the presence of seven Italian Communists in the European Parliament are signs of a gradually changing attitude. Here, the influence of the rank and file has been noteworthy. Moreover, it is obvious that the small, uninfluential parties stick to the doctrinaire refusal of any integration movement, whereas the French and the Italian mass parties show an increasing flexibility. This was clearly apparent during the Communist conference held in London in January 1971, where the six parties conferred with those of the four candidate countries. On that occasion, a rather striking interview of Sgr. Giorgio Amendola, MP appeared in the *Morning Star*, in which the Italian leader advocated 'democratization' of the Community and, specifically, direct elections for the European Parliament. Moreover, he declared himself in favour of British membership, because of the progressive contribution the Labour Party would be able to make.

Outside the political extremes on both sides however, there is apparent unanimity as to the desirability of European co-operation, integration or even Federation of some kind. Still, this unanimity in words sometimes does not go beyond lip service.

Consequently it may worthwhile analysing some of the plans put forward in this field, and seeing what they have in common, where they dissent. From the outset it should be noted that there is a considerable margin between what could be said in different periods by 'Europeans' of different creed. For instance, in 1950, even Gaullists seemed to go fairly on the road of integration, whereas today, 'supranationality' seems to have become a dirty word.

On the other hand, it is interesting to note that some politicians who are widely apart in internal politics, sometimes reach similar conclusions when 'Europe' is at stake. By contrast, party friends can strongly disagree on issues connected with Federalism. In fact, such terms as 'Right' and 'Left' have to be re-interpreted fundamentally in matters connected with European Union, where nation-bound Socialists can be less progressive than Conservatives who favour radical supranational change.

Finally, we should bear in mind that there is a strong link between the foreign policy one would like to see a United Europe pursue and the institutional set-up such a policy requires.

II. We will leave aside the numerous schemes envolved by isolated statesmen, philosophers or poets before 1941[1]. Their value is purely academic, since they never reached the point where an idea becomes a policy. Perhaps mention should be made in passing, of the Holy Alliance[2], which tried to set up an institutionalized system of 'summit meetings' between European princes and leading statesmen, after

Waterloo. Launched by Czar Alexander Ist, it had lofty ideals at the outset, but rapidly declined after it had become an anti-Liberal machine in favour of political 'status quo'.

It was not until 1929 that a Foreign Secretary took up the idea officially. On 11th of September of that year, Aristide Briand, speaking for France but knowing that his German colleague Dr. Gustav Stresemann would agree with him, made a speech in the Assembly of the League, in Geneva, suggesting that the European States might form a 'federal link' between each other, in the framework of the world-wide organization. Briand's initiative can therefore be considered as the first official 'model' proposed.

Asked to elaborate his plan in greater detail, he – or rather his Secretary General Alexis Léger, who used to sign his poetry under the name of Saint John Perse – composed a memorandum which was circulated to all European League members.

The answers given by each of them are enlightening. They reflect polite agreement 'in principle' on the one hand, and a great deal of mental reservations on the other. It seems as if each country approached the problem from the point of view of its own particular interests. The small ones considered 'Federation' as a means to escape domination by their more powerful neighbours. The defeated States saw it as a pretext to bring about revision of the much hated peace treaties. The so-called 'winners' of Versailles, by contrast, wanted to use it as a guarantee of the frontiers as they were. All however, claimed that they were speaking in favour of European peace and security, of a better balance in international relations, of closer co-operation and more friedly agreement among all concerned.

Moreover, three fundamental questions arose:
- first: what to do with the League of Nations after the United States or Europe had been formed? In fact, the forerunner of UNO was still overwhelmingly European in its membership, since neither the United States nor (till 1934) the Soviet Union were members, and its seat remained located in Europe;
- secondly, how could the United Kingdom belong to an exclusively European club, since she was the heart of a world-wide, multiracial Empire and Commonwealth?
- thirdly: would not the US resent the creation of a 'paneuropean' union, the power of which would put America's Federation in the shadow, especially since several European States, for instance France, administered large colonial territories?

13

However, these objections never had a chance to be thoroughly discussed, since the Briand plan failed almost immediately.

After Stresemann's death, shortly after the Assembly meeting, the German government changed its attitude. It tried very hard to outflank the rising popularity of the Nazis, and believed it could do so in pursuing a disturbingly nationalistic policy of its own. Briand himself gradually lost most of his influence at home. More important, the economic depression which set in at the same time, gave rise to protectionist reactions which ran counter to any European union scheme. Finally, the French memorandum killed its own impetus in stating that, although a sort of 'United States of Europe' was desirable, national sovereignty should in no case be restricted[3]. It probably was inevitable that the plan should be watered down in that manner. But reassuring the nationalists meant taking the teeth out of the so-called 'Federation'. In conclusion we can only say that this first 'model' was a vague and ineffective one.

III. During the war, the Nazis made a considerable propaganda effort in misusing the word 'Europe'. Let us see what their 'model' – the second one we come across – stood for. They put it forward in an effort to recruit volunteers for the Eastern front and tried to appeal to a sort of cultural idealism: our center of secular civilization should not be overrun by 'bolshevik, Asiatic barbarians'. . .

However, Hitler never made any real effort to propose a blueprint for the 'New Order' he promised and which, he said, would emerge from the war after the inevitable German victory. Realistically, he even dismissed the idea of a German empire, to be surrounded by satellite States. 'Satellites', he rightly thought, would instinctively look for more national autonomy and, thereby, create trouble, whereas sheer puppet governments would be useless, since they would not have any impact on local public opinion. Therefore, direct rule by Germany was preferable. In the East, the Slav population, being 'subhuman', would be exterminated or sent into exile in far away steppes. In the West, the 'Germanic' peoples, such as the Dutch, the Flemings and possibly the Scandinavians, would be further 'germanized', by persuasion and force. In short, Hitler never envisaged any real Federation, not even under German hegemony. He dreamt solely of a full-fledged denationalization of all nations, apart from the dominating Germans.

However, this was not how some of the more honest 'collaborators' understood the situation. When they used the word 'Europe', they

14

sometimes, sincerely but naively, thought of a plurinational, economically and politically united Continent, where national frontiers would have disappeared, but national differentiations be respected. In short, they visualized a United Europe of a hegemonistic type, a 'pax Germanica' comparable to the Roman rule. After all, had not Hitler's Minister for Foreign trade, Herr Funk (called 'Rundfunk' because of his frequent travels) been the first to coin the phrase 'European Economic Community'?

Sometimes the collaborators even put forward arguments that had been familiar to the Paneuropean Movement, which Count Coudenhove-Kalergi had created in 1924. Some examples illustrate this similarity.

On the one hand, Russian membership of a European Federation had always been ruled out by Kalergi. He, in fact, thought of the Soviet-Union – not in terms of anarchy and utopia, as was common in that early period – but of continental power and military threat.

On the other, he never believed that the relationship between continental 'Paneurope' and Great-Britain could be more than one of good neighbourhood, since London's policy had constantly aimed at keeping the European States apart and, if possible, even in a state of permanent rivalry.

During the occupation, men like the Belgian collaborator Pierre Daye took up some of these arguments. But he definitely abandoned the basis of democracy, which had been Kalergi's. He thought that the democrats had ample chances to achieve what history required from them, namely to promote European Union. The democratic epigones had failed to do so, and, consequently, their enemy was to accomplish in his own style, what had been left undone. Even if one had misgivings about certain aspects of National Socialism, Daye said, one had to acknowledge that the dies were cast: Hitler did what 'Paneurope' had hoped for in vain. Not few intellectuals, even from the previous Left, were seduced by this seemingly realistic argumentation[4]. Where democratic Federalism had failed, authoritarian Hegemony would succeed in a task which, anyhow, was placed on History's agenda.

By contrast, the 'model' which the non-Communist resistance-fighters put forward – our third one – was of an entirely different nature[5]. As far as they were not politically neutral Patriots – men whose ambitions did not go beyond the aim of national liberation – most of them thought in terms of Socialism and European unity. Still strongly

Europe-oriented, they considered the peace of our Continent to be the key to peace at large. The impressive manifesto they drafted in Geneva, where representatives of nine national underground movements (inclusing Germany's) came together in 1944, beautifully illustrates this lucid way of thinking.

Starting from the fact that all European nations had participated in the struggle against Hitler, they suggested that the occupied countries had a right to participate in the shaping of a new society. Should a world-wide league be set up again? Surely. But the lack of cohesion between Continents and civilizations, so different from one another and so much torn apart by ideological rift, would preclude the success of any institution comparable to the one that had so lamentably failed in Geneva. The solution, therefore, lay in a universal organization based upon regional groups instead of individual nations[6].

Most of these ideas had been advocated with particular vigour by the Italian Federalists who, under the guidance of men like Altiero Spinelli and Ernesto Rossi, had developed a seriously worked-out model as early as 1943. This document took the title of 'Manifesto di Ventotene', after the name of the island where they had been kept prisoners under Fascist rule[7]. Since the Italian Movimento Federalista Europeo was to play an important part in the shaping of Federalism after the war, we have to dwell on it for a while.

The early Spinelli 'model' took its main inspiration in the experience of American Federalism. It was strongly anti-functionalist and considered the problem of European integration as essentially political, even constitutional. Since the seventeen eighties, the method for uniting independent States was well-known: a Constituent Assembly had to be convened, and the Constitution this gathering would work out had to be ratified by popular vote in the participating countries. During that campaign, it would be the task of the Federalists to win over public opinion, as Madison, Hamilton and Jay had done in their famous *Federalist Letters,* a classic in our field.

IV. The European Union of Federalists, founded in Paris in December 1946, had chosen its title carefully. In a way, it can be considered the heir to both the Resistance movements and the Ventotene manifesto. Still, there were considerable differences between Spinelli's views and the EUF's. What exactly did the EUF understand by the universally accepted catchword of 'Federalism'?

16

During its initial phase it was far from accepting the purely European and purely constitutionalist approach which the Italians put forward. Its first leadership considered 'Federalism' in a much wider sense and therefore had rejected the idea of calling the organization 'Union of European Federalists'. In fact, it saw European integration as only one consequence – be it probably the most important one – of Federalist doctrine in general. Consequently, a different, a fourth 'model' arose, which has been called 'integral Federalism'.

On its stationery, it had printed its leading principle: 'l'Europe uni dans un Monde uni', and it immediately took up contact with representatives of World-Federalist organizations. True, this co-operation did not last. When the 'radical' atmosphere of the immediate post-war months had disappeared and Winston Churchill had launched his very moderate 'United Europe Committee', the EUF was rapidly drawn into the maelstrom of political manoeuvering and compromising. Its 'revolutionary' impetus was gradually lost. None the less, it succeeded in introducing a way of thinking that was new and could not remain without effect. In fact, it was to bear fruit in the early 1950's when the Community of the Six emerged from Robert Schuman's initiative.

The basic post-war document of the Federalists dates from before the official foundation of EUF. It is the 'Hertenstein declaration', which came out in September 1946, just when Churchill made his resounding speech at the University of Zurich. At Hertenstein, a small tourist village on the Lake of Lucerne, a tiny international group of 'militants' met, nearly all of them without having behind them more than a very limited number of registered members[8].

Still, the final resolution of Hertenstein contained a few principles which were to guide the European movement as it grew. Here is our fourth 'model', after Briand's, Hitler's and the one the Italian Anti-Fascists had had in mind. True, the link between Hertenstein and the Italian Resistance is obvious, but in Hertenstein the interpretation of 'Federalism' is more explicit.

Of course, the first principle was the definite acceptance of Federalism as such, especially as regards supranational institutions to be set up in Europe. But article 2 showed that, for those who had subscribed to the declaration, this concept meant more than just a transfer of sovereignty. Federalism, for them, constituted a general philosophy of democratic order, where power would not be concentrated at the summit, but conceded from below. In practice, this meant that the movement would never advocate the creation of a European or a

World State, entrusted with supreme authority in all civil affairs. It meant that local matters should be dealt with locally, that a European government should arbitrate between individual countries, and that an intercontinental authority should be responsible exclusively for world affairs. In article 10 it was specified that 'regional unions' within the European union were welcome in so far as they had been concluded freely and corresponded to a need. This was a blessing given to Benelux, then 'in statu nascendi'.

A second principle, closely related to the first, was that the European Union to be formed should not be considered as directed against anybody. It should refrain from power-political dreams, but at the same time, be strong enough to resist attempts to make Europe anybody's satellite. It would be a regional union in the sense of article 52 of the UN Charter.

In so doing, Europe would prove that the 'spirit of Federalism' was able to contribute to the birth of a harmonious, well-balanced, universal union-for-peace.

Once the EUF was founded and had to define its practical policy, its first move was to approach Soviet diplomats, in order to persuade Moscow that a European Union which would include both West and East Europe, would be the best guarantee of the USSR's legitimate desire for security. Of course, the Soviet Union would find it possible, even easy, to occupy the countries East of what came to be called the 'Iron Curtain'. But this would mean that the West would, by necessity, fall into the American orbit, whereas the 'Popular Democracies' would constantly resent their status of satellites. On two occasions the author went to Prague in order to form a local group, able and willing to take the lead of a Continent-wide movement which would aim at making an 'integral Europe'. Such a 'Switzerland of the World' would be federal, militarily neutral and outward-looking to both sides.

This 'model' was of course short-lived. The EUF was unable to create a mass-movement in favour of its program. The British Labour-government showed no interest in Europe or Federalism. The Soviet-Union preferred satellites rather than allies. And a second visit to Czechoslovakia in the summer of 1948 proved that this country had already mentally surrendered to the fate that was to befall her in February 1948.

V. This initial Federalist conception having failed, the EUF had a

18

choice, either to disband, or to work for Federalism within the limited framework of what could only be a West European Union. Its first regular congress, held in Montreux in the summer of 1947, decided to continue action 'provisionally without the East, but not against it'[9]. This Rubicon having been crossed, one problem became burning: the relationship with the Churchillian 'United Europe Movement'. What was the 'model' of that group?

The Zurich speech which we mentioned earlier, had been concluded with an appeal to the Europeans: 'Europe arise!'. But what did Churchill mean in practice? To what extent could he become an ally of the Federalists? How should both movements co-operate? Hardly any session of the EUF's Central Committee was held in those days without this question being hotly debated. Even today, the discussion is not entirely closed: Denis de Rougemont recently expressed the opinion that if the Federalists had kept their hands clean, and refused any collaboration with the Conservative leader, they would have won in the end. Neither this nor the opposite can be proven, but it is easy to define the points where the two groups dissented.

The first concerned the attitude to be taken vis-à-vis the Soviet Union and the Communist-lead countries. Here however, Churchill won an easy victory, since the brutal way in which the bolshevization of the Eastern States proceeded, was only too eloquent. Rapidly, all Europeans, Left or Right, came to realize that Stalin had installed a totalitarian regime from which there was no escape. None the less, the militantly anti-Communist line of Churchill's continued to shock the Federalists. 'United Europe' gradually became a means to preserve the social 'status quo'. At least this appeared to be the case.

The second point concerned the institutional form a 'United Europe' should take. Here, Churchill had only two suggestions to make: organic reconciliation between Germany and her former allies, especially France – and the creation of a 'Council of Europe'. No mention was made of supranationality, and the UE Committee limited its declarations to vague assertions about 'pragmatic approach' and 'leaving the future open'. In practice, this anti-dogmatism meant that national sovereignty was to be considered sacrosanct.

Thirdly, the participation of Britain as a full member of a United Europe remained unclear, to say the least. The immense prestige

Churchill enjoyed at that time made many over-enthusiastic Continentals miss some meaningful sentences of the Zurich-speech. However, at unbiased reading, they were embarrassing enough: 'Great-Britain, the British Commonwealth of Nations, mighty America, and I trust Soviet Russia – for then indeed all would be well – must be the friends and sponsors of the new Europe and must champion its rights to live and shine'. 'Friends and sponsors': not 'members', since even Britain was to stay out! The Europeans might have spared themselves many disillusions, in later years, had they taken these eloquent but disappointing words at their face-value.

Finally, what was still worse than anything else: Churchill in opposition had called for union, but Churchill in power again after 1951 was to refuse any tangible British support to the European Defence Community which was then under discussion. Not only was British membership out of the question, but the Tory government refused to give a military guarantee to the Pleven-plan. Such a guarantee, similar to the one which was to be given to Western European Union in 1954-1955 might have changed the final vote of the French Parliament. Churchill, however, did not consider such a plea desirable.

None the less, the Churchillian conception – the fifth 'model' if you wish – dominated the sene in the late 'fourties. Since the Cold War had broken out in all its fierceness, the anti-Communist overtones which the European Movement gained in that period, were not unexplainable. They corresponded to the atmosphere of those years, when Paul Henri Spaak, then Belgian Foreign Secretary, made his famous speech in the General Assembly of the United Nations (September 1948), on the theme 'we are afraid' (of Soviet aggression).

The frosty climate that prevailed and the split between the two parts of Europe killed the high hopes and ideals born at Hertenstein. The spirit of Zurich – and of Fulton, where Churchill made his most militant anti-communist speech – corresponded only too well to the situation as it had become. The birth of NATO, in response to the Prague 'coup', definitively brought Western Europe into the American realm. It is difficult to see how this could have been otherwise.

VI.   However, it would be wrong to think that the statesmen, who in the early 'fifties launched the sixth 'model' for a smaller but more tightly knit Europe, would have been unilaterally inspired by anti-Russian motives. Nor were the promoters of the Six anti-British.

Of course, the Soviet menace was still there, or thought to be there. Of course, as long as Stalin was alive, an instinct of self-preservation would drive the Europeans together, whereas his death in March 1953, surely harmed the European movement. But defence was not the primary concern of a man like Jean Monnet. On the contrary, his main preoccupation in the late 'fourties was the opposite: he wanted to launch an initiative, through which public opinion would be distracted from the morbid, sterilizing, cold-war fears and policies[10]. If it were possible, he thought, to show the world that new ideals and new methods could be introduced in the field of international relations, new hopes would arise and military preparations would no longer be supreme in people's minds.

Again, reconciliation between France and Germany would be the key, and Robert Schuman not only accepted this principle, but, as a Lorrain who had been a German citizen for more than thirty years, he gave enthusiastic support to it. 'The pooling of coal and steel production', he said in his famous press declaration of May the 9th 1950, '... will change the destiny of these regions which have been long devoted to the production of arms to which they themselves were the first to fall constantly victim'[11]. Schuman knew what he was talking about, and the pacifist undertone of his speech is clear. There is no Fulton-like mention of Soviet imperialism to be resisted.

As for the French attitude towards Britain, it has sometimes been said that in those days the Continentals indulged in abstract constitution-mongering. Then flaunting their little success with the United Kingdom, they would have gone forward on their own, trying to achieve this doctrinaire utopia.

This interpretation of the facts is based on a misunderstanding. Nobody on the Continent ever wanted or tried to 'exclude' Britain. But during the last months of 1949 it had become obvious that whoever wanted to promote a really united Europe, could do so only with a group of nations willing to pay the price. And that group would, by necessity, be smaller than the membership of the Council or of OEEC.

In the autumn that followed the hopeful Strassbourg summer of 1949, two decisive events took place. On the one hand, Britain devalued sterling by a 'national' decision. Or perhaps it was not that national, since it took place in Washington. In any case, it was taken as if no Strassbourg existed. On the other hand, the first session of the Council's Committee of Ministers could hardly have been more disappointing. All recommendations of the Consultative Assembly had been brushed off the conference-table, and it had become clear that the 'larger' Europe would have to be 'functional', i.e. purely intergovernmental.

In the view of most Continentals, this method could have some effect, but it could not achieve nearly enough. True also, Monnet and Schuman had chosen a limited – in a way precisely a 'functional' – approach to the European problem. They had refrained from indicating any constitutional consequences that might be drawn one day from the coal and steel pool. Some of the more radical Federalists had even thought that Schuman was rather timid in stating that 'A united Europe will not be achieved all at once, not in a single framework: it will be formed by concrete measures which first of all create a solidarity in fact'. But he had underlined that 'supranationality' was a practical necessity if one wanted to go beyond the classical forms of inter-governmentalism. It was a great pity that Britain and the Scandinavian countries should have rejected participation in the Schuman initiative, but they have only themselves to blame, in so far as there is room for blame at all.

In more than one respect one must regret that the Coal and Steel-plan should have been followed so rapidly by another French initiative, the Pleven-plan, which was to become the Treaty for a European Defence Community.

Here again, some misunderstandings have to be cleared up. The Europeans never 'chose' the military field to make their next move towards a Federation. In 1950 they had no choice at all. When the Korean war broke out, the problem of German participation in the military effort of the West became inescapable. The Iron Curtain had become a stable dividing line between the two parts of Europe, and both Germanies had to accept the consequences of this fact, each of them in its own sphere of interest. Moreover, it seemed increasingly ludicrous that the West Germans should remain free of any military obligations, personal or financial. Consequently, it seemed acceptable to re-arm Germans, rather than Germany as a sovereign State.

This having been said, it remains deplorable that the European idea, which had started with the full impetus of radical Pacifism, should from then on have been connected with the future of a rearmament plan, however unavoidable.

VII. What the French call the 'quarrel' of EDC has been an essential episode in the evolution of European Federalism. In fact, this Treaty and the massive American support given to it, once and for all buried an idea that never grew into becoming a real 'model': the idea of

22

Western Europe as a 'third force' between the two blocks. For some time a few Left-wing Federalists tried to promote it, but it was outside reality. From now on, Western Europe had lined up with the United States. Not even de Gaulle's action, to which we will have to return later, gave it a new chance, but some radical Gaullists at least tried to revive it in public opinion (cf. the 'Mouvement pour l'Indépendance européenne').

Of course, the development of the late 40's and the early 50's was not entirely unexpected. The same Robert Schuman who had launched his economic integration plan, had negotiated the NATO treaty during 1948-1949, that is: more than a year before. In his mind, the principle of collective, i.e. Atlantic security had always been supreme, since he remembered that, should it have been adopted in the 'thirties, Hitler might have considered his aggression too risky. But, apart from such considerations, was common defence the only justification of the Alliance?

In those days, the idea of an 'Atlantic Community' – with Europe as an essential partner: our seventh 'model' – was hammered out. Culturally, the peoples around the Ocean had much in common, to develop and to protect[12]. Especially after 30th August 1954, when the French Parliament had defeated EDC, many Europeans asked themselves whether it was still realistic to go on calling for union in their part of the world, or whether a wider, bi-continental scheme was not the more promising. The day of Atlantic Federalism seemed to have arrived.

However, there never was any kind of popular movement in favour of such a solution. Academics wrote books about it[13]. Governments referred to it. Industrialists and bankers wondered whether a United Europe had not already become obsolete as a tool for economic expansion. Conferences were called and speeches made. But the public remained cool. There never was a wide-spread feeling of Atlantic togetherness, not even in the Netherlands, where Continentalism had always been distrusted, and where the links with the Anglosaxon world have always been strong.

By now, the Vietnam war has further deteriorated whatever 'Atlanticism' there was.

Moreover, opinions widely differed as to the institutional forms such an Atlantic Union should take. Not only the greater or lesser degree of Federalism was at stake here, but the more fundamental question as to how the United States was to enter such a union. If it was to maintain its national cohesion, its power would by necessity dominate the group, so that the feelings of pride and collective identity of each European people in a disunited Europe would be hurt. But on the other hand, could anybody expect the Americans to disband their 'more perfect union' so as to enter an Atlantic entity as fifty individual States? The question was never answered not even by Clarence Streit, the most forceful supporter of a 'Federation of the Northern free'[14].

There was however another Atlantic 'model' which seemed more realistic. It was proposed by those Europeans who were directly involved in the integration of their own Continent: men like Monnet. In their view, Europe should hammer out a 'foreign policy' of its own, and then approach the American Allies so as to earn their agreement. The US should be approached, they thought, not as future confederates but as actual partners. Far from being afraid that a strong European Community would hamper Atlantic solidarity, they considered that the main obstacle on the way to it lay precisely in the inferiority complex of the Europeans. For this disease, a Continental Federation was to be the best cure. Both from the economic and the political point of view, there was no danger that the Europeans, once united, would go it alone. Independence, even Continental, was out of the question anyway. By contrast: as long as the European nations stuck to the fiction of national sovereignty, their decadence would be inevitable – and the Americans would be blamed for it, unjustly but bitterly.

A new impetus was given to the idea of Atlantic partnership when, in August 1961, Britain asked for admission to the Common Market. If the negotiations should succeed – and many observers were over-optimistic about the issue – EEC would cease to be unilaterally 'continental'. An Anglosaxon nation would join it, thus bringing America closer to Europe, and vice-versa. It seemed as if a new perspective was opened, and Professor U. W. Kitzinger voiced many people's convictions when he wrote in 1963: 'There is every reason to believe that the free world would be helped by a strong, united Europe, able to stand by the side of the United States ... Americans would no longer feel themselves alone in the world with a few sometimes recalcitrant retainers, but see themselves as one half of a partnership between Europe and America – in which America need not even, in some years, be the leading half'[15].

On the Western side of the Ocean, this concept found its expression in President Kennedy's 'Grand Design', in his 'independence'-speech at Philadelphia, and in the Trade Expansion Act, the campaign for which was opened on December the 6th, 1961. No longer, the President

24

declared, would there be any 'special relations' between the English-speaking countries, but in their place would come an infinitely more ambitious system of organized solidarity between the Atlantic nations. Concretely, the US was prepared to do away with any tariffs laid on products, at least 80% of the trade in which was in the hands of the Atlantic group, i.e. the US and the enlarged Community taken together[16].

Unfortunately, Britain's entry was vetoed twice, and thereby, the range of products hinted at by Kennedy, remained negligible. None the less, the President restated his vision of Atlantic partnership on the 25th of June 1963, less than half a year after de Gaulle's press conference. In the St. Paul's church at Frankfort he said: 'It is only a fully cohesive Europe that can protect us all against fragmentation of the Alliance. Only such a Europe will permit full reciprocity of treatment across the Ocean in the face of the Atlantic agenda. With only such a Europe can we have a full give-and-take between equals, an equal sharing of responsibilities, and an equal level of sacrifice'.

VIII. Even then, these words of Kennedy sounded somewhat unrealistic in the ears of many Europeans who had welcomed the 'Interdependence'-speech with great expectations. Now, Britain had been rebuked and France was withdrawing from NATO.

What concepts did the French President bring to European integration? What was his 'model' concerning Europe's relations with East and West? How did he influence the internal development of the Community, which had started action precisely during the same fateful year 1958, when the Fourth Republic fell and the Fifth came into being?

In 1957, the small Gaullist group in the National Assembly had voted against the Treaty of Rome, the general philosophy of which it had disliked ('l'Europe de Monsieur Monnet'). It was therefore logical that the promoters of integration should have watched the events in Paris with great concern. Was not de Gaulle going to tear the Treaty to pieces and set up a 'national economy' along protectionist lines? The real outcome, however, has proved to be more complex. Several factors have to be remembered here, some encouraging, others disruptive[17].

First: the General, for all his emotional Nationalism ('la France vient du fond des âges'. . .), had never been in favour of high tariffs. He despised the petty-bourgeois attitude of so many French employers who preferred quietly earned dividends to creative risks. French genius, he

thought, should be able, not only to face foreign competition successfully, but even to conquer a partner's home-market.

Moreover, he saw that French agriculture would benefit from an
opening-up of the frontiers. Consequently, he was to insist on the
necessity for EEC, to complement free trade in industry by wider commercial horizons for French farmers. Paradoxically enough, the states-
man who most consistently opposed supranational developments, was
constantly on the Commission's side when 'green Europe' was at stake.

During the first half of his presidency – roughly as long as France's
hands were tied by the Algerian war – the positive factors were predominant, whereas the emphasis on fundamental anti-Federalism became supreme from 1962 onward.

The General's 'model' of European union – the ninth we have to
look into – was a real one. His interest in the matter was not only
verbal. Nor did it date from the days when others had already put the
movements into action. A few weeks before Churchill's Zurich-speech,
in an address given at Bar-le-Duc, he had advocated a scheme for co-
operation, based of course on each country's national sovereignty. He
never wavered on that principle, but he did have the intuition of a
plurinational civilization to be defended and revived.

It is perhaps useful to summarize his ideas in three of his favourite
'formulas'. They are:
– 'Europe of the States' (emphatically not 'of the fatherlands', as is
  often thought, since he discarded this expression in so many words);
  this meant that 'union' stood for 'political union' and that, at least
  for a long time to come, only States had the political power to decide
  and implement their decisions: consequently, the European Commission had to be considered as a single team of experts (although it
  deserved high praise in that respect, particularly when its conclusions
  reinforced the French 'dossier');
– 'European Europe': this meant that the Atlantic dream had been
  swept aside: admittedly, only America could have imposed supranational schemes on a group of reluctant European nations, but such
  an intervention from outside would have been disastrous for the
  cause of unity itself; in de Gaulle's oratory, 'supranationality' is
  curiously enough equated with American domination, although it has
  often been advocated with good reasons that only a strong supranational Europe can hope for relative independence;
– 'Europe to the Ural': this meant that for too long Europe had been
  considered as merely Western-Europe: on the basis of selfdetermina-

tion and in the perspective of political and military blocks being broken up, close co-operation should be established between all Europeans, anxious to maintain or regain their national identity and freedom; the invasion of Czechoslovakia made this perspective doubtful; moreover, the Russians disliked such a geographical limitation of 'Europe', through which their Asian provinces seemed to be relegated to the 'Asian' realm of China.

Finally, it might be said that a fourth 'idée-force' – or rather an axioma – seemed to underlie the Gaullist doctrine, although it has never been publicly expressed in so many words, namely, the spiritual and therefore political supremacy of the French genius, its calling to be Europe's hegemonist. In fact, it does not seem unjust to suppose that de Gaulle considered the Franco-German agreement of January 1963 – it was published a few days after Britain's rebuke – as the juridical basis for a condominium between the two greatest powers among the Six. However, history has shown that two States do not by necessity follow the same political lines, just because they are the biggest. In fact, the agreement had hardly any political effect at all, especially since Dr. Adenauer had to leave the German scene.

After April 1969 the Gaullist government has applied the fundamentals of the Gaullist doctrine with much more flexibility, but it still has to reckon with strong doctrinaire feelings among its supporters. To date, President Pompidou's suggestions in the European field are so 'pragmatic', that it is difficult to see what they mean in practice.

IX. As for the Communities themselves, it is not easy to spell out the exact 'model', the tenth, which they on their part, want to see achieved. After 1954, the Coal and Steel Community had to live in a political climate that hardly permitted any radical supranational interpretations of the Paris Treaty, whereas, at a later stage, Euratom was killed, or at least seriously curtailed, by the French decision not to endow it with the country's nuclear equipment. As for the Common Market, which was successful in more than one field, it could hardly have invented a coherent philosophy of its own, since it had to fight a day-to-day battle in order to maintain whatever 'communitarian' content it was allowed to display. Still fairly ambitious in principle, it had to become more and more 'pragmatic', so that it has even been said that, in reality, it was technocratic in its philosophy.

Up to a certain point, this analysis is not incorrect. Since the European Commission is far from being a Continental government, and the

Council of Ministers is not subject to any sort of democratic control, the Parliament of the Six is hardly less 'consultative' than the Assembly of the Council of Europe. Consequently, whatever integration is achieved, is carried out in the course of 'marathon'-sessions, on the basis of expertise and negotiation skill. This is far from ideal, but at present even direct elections for the Strassbourg-Parliament would not alter the fact that this gathering of national MP's has no responsible government to discuss its problems with. In those circumstances, any hope of a rapid democratization – that is: federalization – of EEC has to remain platonic, as long as no fresh wave of European action appears.

For the time being, the Community is therefore uncomfortably seated between two stools. It is not an inter-governmental organization of the classical type. It is surely not a Confederacy of a pre-Federal organism such as described in juridical textbooks. In a way, it is an institutional monster, which cannot satisfy anybody.

Probably, things would have been different if the 'spill-over' process, which surely is built into the Community-system, would have been allowed to develop, as many observers have predicted it would. But this process has been hampered or even stopped by more than one national government in the course of time. Especially the French government under de Gaulle has made anti-Federalism an integral part of France's official doctrine.

In these circumstances, it is understandable that some outstanding neo-functionalists should have concluded that, purely technical moves being the only possibility left open, all dreams about political integration should have been abandoned a long time ago. They blame the Community for blurring the issues through its unceasing, irritating attempt to achieve goals it is no longer, or not yet, suited for.

This seems to be the attitude of Professor Frans Alting von Geusau, whose important book *Beyond the European Community*[18] comes to the conclusion that the Common Market, trying to 'pursue two hares', missed both. Neither did it modestly and competently set up a total free trade area protected by a not too high common tariff, nor did it contribute to more harmonious international relations. Too Federalist to be functional and too limited in its instrumentality to become the nucleus of a new Continental world-power, it never made up its mind as to what it was meant to be. Thereby it failed.

Whatever one may think of Alting von Geusau's criticism in detail, one cannot help wondering whether it is not an illusion to think that national economies could be integrated 'leaving political considerations

28

aside', as he seems to have wished. Today, any economy, national or continental, has to be manipulated, and in this field 'manipulation' implies a number of political choices to be made. This at least, de Gaulle knew perfectly well ('On fait de la politique, quand'. . . etc.). This Professor Hallstein also knew[19], but they drew different consequences from their statement. Whereas the former concluded that the national, sovereign States had to remain supreme, the latter underlined the absolute necessity of a transfer, a pooling of political sovereignty.

This debate will continue all along the evolution of the Community, since it reflects the present situation in Europe, i.e. both the imperative necessity of integration and the obstinacy of the nations not to have their independence limited.

Consequently, if we want to find a coherent, theoretically thought-out 'model' of European union, the most successful of all European organizations will be the least able to produce it. Or rather, this 'model' reflects the lack of decision which characterizes the present situation: 'Yes . . . no . . . and yet . . . perhaps'.

X. Even so, one fact remains: EEC is not concerned with economic activities, such as production, banking or trade – it is merely integrating social and economic *policies*. It therefore seems confusing to present 'political union' as an entirely different matter, quite apart from what the Common Market tries to do. Still, a problem of political integration remains, even outside the range of social and economic affairs, however political in themselves. For this field, the expression 'political politics' has been coined, but it is perhaps clearer to stick to the traditional word 'diplomacy'.

At the Saarbrücken-congress of the German Social-Democratic Party, Federal Chancellor Willy Brandt said that this country could no longer remain 'an economic giant and a political dwarf'. The same is true for the Community, which, even without Britain, already constitutes the biggest trading bloc in the world. It is therefore shocking to see, that until recently, the six foreign secretaries could discuss any technical subject the Commission submitted to them, whereas 'political' topics such as the situation in the Middle-East remained taboo. Likewise, it is absurd that all trade barriers should be done away with, whereas each of the Community members still thinks fit to organize its 'national' defence, its logistics and the supply of its military equipment. Surely, defence has no place in the Treaty of Rome, but the absence of a military corollary of EEC is an anomaly which only the downfall of EDC in 1954 can explain.

Some writers and politicians have stepped into this vacuum and elaborated what might be called our eleventh 'model'. The most forceful among them is the leader of the Bavarian Christian-Social Union, Herr Franz-Josef Strauss, who advocates the creation of a European Federation on the basis of a common army and, more specifically, a common nuclear weapon[20]. His argumentation is shared by Prof. Hallstein and perhaps by many others, who are careful not to express themselves in too concrete terms, since the subject is complex and highly unpopular.

Doubtless, Strauss is a European Federalist, and this point alone should have sufficed to spare him the title which some of his opponents gave him too readily: the title of being a 'German Gaullist'.

Strauss draws all the conclusions from his political concept. He wants to see a pooling of the British 'striking force' with the French 'force de frappe'. This merger would denationalize the weapon and make the creation of a European government imperative. There cannot be a Federal State without a reasonable amount of security, Strauss says, but vice-versa, no real security in our times can be assured without an atomic umbrella, the use of which should depend exclusively on a European decision-making authority. An alliance with the United States would probably be indispensable for the time being, but NATO should no longer remain an organization of the hegemonistic type: it should become a real partnership between equals. In other words, what Monnet and Kennedy looked forward to in economic matters, Strauss wants to see in the field of defence and, consequently, in diplomacy. He advocates a 'European Europe' (here we find again a certain Gaullist terminology), but surely not organized along the lines of the weak intergovernmental model, de Gaulle proposed in the Fouchet-plans[21].

In the military chapter of his book, *Sicherheit für Europa,* the author explains how he fully realized the hopeless dependence of today's Europe in 1956, when it became clear that France and Britain together were unable to achieve their common operation in Egypt. Only a Federal Europe, built up around a European Defence Community, including the control over weapons of mass-destruction, Strauss considers to be a realistic solution. Where the Pacifists have failed – like the 1848-Liberals failed to promote German unity, leaving the job to be done by Bismarck – a harsher kind of thinking will become imperative for Europe now.

As far as we can see, hardly any attempt has been made to challenge the logic of Strauss' suggestions. They have been rejected indignantly by many, but so far the European Left has not taken the trouble to draft convincing counterproposals in the field of defence and security[22]. Up till now, most opponents have wrongly considered that a negative answer was a policy. Unfortunately, a refusal, however justified in itself, cannot take the place of a program.

XI. Nearly all the preceding 'models' seem to take it for granted that 'Europe' means 'Western Europe', the Six, an enlarged Community or at the utmost the Council of Europe group. True, the first post-war Federalists, as we saw, never thought in purely Western terms, until the hard facts of Stalinism obliged them to do so. But for a long time, the only consideration given to the countries East of the Iron Curtain, could hardly go beyond lip services paid to emigré groups. Recently, however, the subject seems to have become debatable again.

By February 1948, the subjection of Eastern Europe to Soviet rule had been completed. Moreover, the Soviet government answered the Marshall-plan by setting up the COMECON. Surely, this institution has changed in character since the days of Stalin, when it was a channel through which ruthless exploitation of the Satellites by the USSR was organized. With some success Rumania has tried to achieve a certain amount of national independence. Yet, COMECON remains an organization of the hegemonistic type, be it only by the weight of its strongest member: it is telling that the secretariat has been established in Moscow.

However, can it be claimed that Russia's economic, military and political triumph has brought great fortune to anybody, including the Russians themselves?

Immediately after Stalin's death in March 1953, a series of risings started with the East German revolt in June. Three years later, the 'Polish October' was followed by the Hungarian insurrection. Then it was the turn of the Poles again, who were followed by the Czechoslovak 'spring' in the late 'sixties. As to the Rumanians, they gradually tried to broaden their breathing space, ably playing off the Soviets against the Chinese. As to the post-1956 Hungarians, they introduced a number of economic and social reforms that were similar to the ones Ota Sik wanted to achieve in his country. Finally, the last weeks of 1970 saw the workers' rising in the Baltic cities of Poland, the fall of Gomulka, and Gierek's timid attempts to liberalize his regime.

In conclusion, the warnings given to Moscow, not to subdue its satellites but to leave them with a reasonable amount of freedom – even in the enlightened interest of the USSR itself – have been disregarded, but the discouraging results are before us today. In many respects, the 'glacis'-countries have become a burden rather than an asset for the USSR, and one wonders how a way-out can be found that would bring acceptable solutions to all concerned. Could not the Federal idea serve a purpose here too, and what could the role of the Common Market become in such an evolution?

These questions were put at a colloquium at Bruges in March 1969, and the broad lines of a possible solution, a twelfth and final 'model', traced. They are already indicated in the title[23]: 'The Popular Democracies after Prague: Hegemony – Nationalism – Integration'. Here follow the main elements of the scheme put forward there and then:
- the 'satellites' want a substantial amount of autonomy, and it is difficult to see how democrats could not sympathize with such a request;
- however, the idea of 'national sovereignty' is outdated; at a moment when the world discovers its inevitable 'interdependence', Nationalism is no longer the answer;
- consequently, an Economic Community might be envisaged in the East, definitely on the basis of public ownership, but with a far greater amount of economic competition and local initiative than was permitted in the framework of purely bureaucratic planning of the authoritarian type;
- such an East-European EC would act as entity like EEC did during the Kennedy Round; it would be linked to the USSR, but not be teleguided by it, just as its Western counterpart, while not having its headquarters in Washington, entertains friendly relations with the US;
- the two European Communities could establish confederal links between each other, possibly through the Council of Europe, whose task would probably be fulfilled if the Six became Ten (or more).

No doubt, this 'model' seems utopian at present. Perhaps it will not remain so, since the alternative is sure to be constant strife, whereas the problem of German dualism would remain unsolved indefinitely.

XII. For the moment, none of the conceptions outlined above[24] corresponds to either all the requirements of the future or the realities of the present. However, the only chance to bring about change lies with the Community. It is engaged now in at least three ambitious schemes. These plans are certainly not going ahead with great inspiration. However, they are there. We may mention them in conclusion:

– the enlargement of EEC through the adhesion of the four candidates: Britain, Ireland, Denmark and Norway; each of these applications poses specific problems, but the case of the United Kingdom is the key, since it is difficult to believe that any other candidate, with the possible exception of Denmark, would maintain its application if the main partner should drop out; however, if the number of EEC-members should grow substantially, it is difficult to see how the present institutional set-up could be sufficient to deal with the additional difficulties that the Ten would have to face; a strengthening of the Executive would therefore become imperative, but for the time being nobody, neither the Six nor the Four – nor even the Commission itself – dares to ask the relevant questions; the present state of British public opinion surely does not permit great expectations in the institutional field; still, efficiency and democratization, which the British will have at heart, might make a strengthening of the framework inescapable;

– the qualitative step to be taken by the Six, in proceeding from their still incomplete customs union to a full-fledged economic and monetary union, according to paragraph 8 of the communiqué of The Hague and as elaborated in the Werner-plan; in fact, if such a union can be achieved in the course of the 1970's, national sovereignty will find itself severely curtailed at the end of the transitional period; this however, can hardly be admitted publicly, especially not in France, where the party in power still maintains nationalistic overtones; it seems fair to say that probably Britain would also insist on not defining the final institutional machinery at too early a stage, but would proceed 'pragmatically' from one stage to the next;

– the problem of 'political' (or rather 'diplomatic') union has been brought up in The Hague (paragraph 15 of the communiqué), and a commission under the chairmanship of a Belgian high civil servant Viscount Davignon, has submitted a draft; on paper this proposal seems to be even less progressive than the best version of the Fouchet-plan which was under discussion in 1961-1962; however, a meeting of the six Foreign Secretaries at Munich in November 1969, showed that a surprising amount of convergence existed among the participants, concerning the problems of the Middle East; this is a new phenomenon, however one may judge the content of the agreement; it has even been decided that, at a later stage, common instructions could be given to the six ambassadors concerned; should this practice become effective in the years to come, it would be only logical that the diplomatic services of the Community-countries be merged into one; but such a perspective is still very far ahead.

Consequently, the chances of European union do not seem too bad at present. But perhaps this is merely apparent, since public opinion – while basically more and more favourable to integration – seems to be shifting to other problems which it begins to consider more essential. This is especially the case among the younger generation, which regards itself as being already 'beyond the European Community'. It no doubt does not realize the enormous amount of nationalistic, or simply conservative, traditional resistance, put up by the national States and their administrations. In fact, national States are still extremely powerful vested interests, perhaps the most powerful of all, although by no means the most efficient. By contrast, pro-Europeans have too often and too readily described the integration-process as having reached and crossed the 'point of no return'. They have therefore suggested, wrongly, that it was becoming more or less automatic and inevitable. Surely there is an inherent force of self-perpetuation and self-expansion in the EEC-machine as in any human machine, but the constant repetition of this fact creates a false atmosphere of optimism, which is not justified and consequently paralyses the more 'revolutionary' antinationalistic energies.

REFERENCES

1. Rolf Helmut Foerster, *Europa, Geschichte einer politischen Idee,* München, Nymphenburger Verlagshandlung 1967.
2. Jacques-Henri Pirenne, *La Sainte-Alliance, Organisation européenne de la Paix mondiale,* Neuchâtel, La Bâconnière, 1946-1949, 2 volumes.
3. B. Mirkine-Guetzevitch et Georges Scelle, *L'Union Européenne,* Paris, Delagrave, 1931 (contains the main documents on the Briand initiative).
4. Pierre Daye, *L'Europe aux Européens,* Bruxelles, Nouvelle Société d'Editions, 1942.
5. *Europa-Föderationspläne der Widerstandsbewegungen, 1940-1945,* Eine Dokumentation gesammelt und eingeleitet von Walter Lipgens, München, R. Oldenbourg Verlag, 1968.
6. Various authors, *L'Europe de Demain,* Neuchâtel, La Bâconnière, 1945 (contains some essays, and the main documents, including the Geneva-manifesto). Cf. Hubert Halin, *L'Europe Unie Objectif Majeur de la Résistance,* Paris/Bruxelles, Editions de l'Union des Résistants pour l'Europe Unie, 1967.

7. Altiero Spinelli. *Manifesto dei Federalisti Europei,* Parma, Ugo Guanda, 1957. Also cf. of the same author; *L'Europe non cade dal Cielo,* Bologna, Il Mulino, 1960.
8. The Hertenstein-manifesto has been reproduced in the author's *L'Idée Européenne,* 1920-1970, Bruges, De Tempel, 1970.
9. The author's speech at the EUF-conference at Montreux (1947) in *Vingt Ans d'Europe,* Bruges, De Tempel, 1966.
10. Erling Bjøl, *La France devant l'Europe, La politique européenne de la IVème République,* Copenhague, Munksgaard, 1966.
11. English translation of Schuman's speech, together with many other essential documents in French and English, in *Landmarks in European Unity – Jalons dans l'Europe Unie,* edited by S. Patijn, Leyden, Sijthoff, 1970, p. 47. Concerning the origin of the Schuman-plan: Robert Schuman, *Pour l'Europe,* Paris, Nagel, 1964, and Jean Monnet, *Les Etats-Unis d'Europe ont commencé,* Paris, 1953.
12. Ernst Bieri, Henri Brugmans, Milorad Drachkovitch, Hans Kohn and Léo Moulin, *Valeurs de Base de la Communauté Atlantique,* Leyden, Sijthoff, 1961.
13. One of the latest and finest: W. Randolph Burgess and James Robert Huntley, *Europe and America, The next ten Years,* New York, Waler & Cy, 1970.
14. Clarence Streit, *Union Now, The Proposal for Inter-Democracy Federal Union,* New York-London, Harper & Bros., 1940.
15. U. W. Kitzinger, *The Politics and Economics of European Integration,* New York, Frederick A. Praeger, 1963, p. 176.
16. George M. Taber, *John F. Kennedy and a Uniting Europe,* Bruges, College of Europe, 1969.
17. Roger Massip, *De Gaulle et l'Europe,* Paris, Flammarion, 1963 and Lord Gladwyn, *De Gaulle's Europe or Why the General said no,* London, Secker & Warburg 1969.
18. Leyden, Sijthoff, 1970. 1812754
19. Walter Hallstein, *United Europe, Challenge & Opportunity,* Cambridge Mass., Harvard University Press and London, Oxford University Press, 1962.
20. Franz-Josef Strauss, *Herausforderung und Antwort,* Stuttgart, Seewald Verlag 1968.
    French translation; *Défi et Réponse, Un programme pour l'Europe,* Paris, Albin Michel, 1969.
21. Robert Bloes, *Le Plan Fouchet et le Problème de l'Europe politique,* Bruges, College of Europe, 1970.
22. The author has made such an attempt in a book which has not been published so far.
23. Jerzy Lukaszewski, editor, *The People's Democracies after Prague,* Bruges, De Tempel, 1970.
24. A valuable attempt to systematize these doctrines, schemes and proposals has been made both by the late André Marchal, *l'Europe Solidaire,* tome I, Paris, Editions Cujas, 1964, tome 2 – *Les Problèmes,* idem, 1970, and by David P. Calleo, *Europe's Future: the Grand Alternatives,* New York, Horizon Press 1965.

An Ostpolitik for the Community

JOHN PINDER

From the European Community's genesis in the Schuman declaration its champions have always seen it as a great political enterprise. The Community might therefore be expected to play some part in dealing with Europe's great political problems. Now it would be hard to deny that the division of Europe between East and West is one of the greatest of these; or that economic matters, in which the Community has its competence, are an important aspect of relations with countries where economics is as highly politicised as it is in Eastern Europe[1] and the Soviet Union. Yet the Community's policy towards these countries has been slight. The member governments have agreed on lists of products freed from import quotas; quotas have been imposed on imports of steel from the East; and certain East European countries have been persuaded to agree not to sell sunflower seed oil, wines and turkeys below the price levels fixed under the Common Agricultural Policy. Why is the discrepancy so wide between the insignificance of these policies and the importance of the problems?

The answer is, of course, that the Community was not allowed to have a substantial policy precisely because the problems were politically so important. His Eastern policy was central to de Gaulle's design of both ending American hegemony over Western Europe and maintaining French hegemony over Germany. Interference by the Community could therefore not be tolerated. At the same time West Germany's relationship with the East has been extremely sensitive, and this would itself have made it hard for the Community to have an Eastern policy[2], even if de Gaulle would have allowed it.

Now, however, de Gaulle is gone and the French government is becoming less anti-communautaire. The Ostpolitik is rendering the Federal Republic's relations with the East much more normal than they were before. These barriers to the formation of a common Community policy have therefore been greatly reduced. The sharp differences that used to characterise the economic policies of West European countries towards Eastern Europe and the Soviet Union, with respect, for example, to credits and import liberalisation, are also much less than they were; and this applies as much to an enlarged Community as to the present Community of six. Bureaucratic inertia and a lack of political will among the member governments will doubtless remain to hinder the development of a Community Ostpolitik. Whether these obstacles are overcome will depend on whether the enlarged Community enjoys a political relance, and on how far the member governments will have grounds to feel they have an interest in a common policy that has substantial weight. The first question is beyond the

39

scope of this paper, which is however designed to throw some light on the second. But before any answer can be ventured, we have to consider the point of view of the Eastern countries and the problems that are inherent in the economic relations between East and West.

EASTERN REACTION TO THE COMMUNITY

There is no equivocation in the attitude of the Russian authorities to the Community. They are against it.

This attitude is supported by their conceptions of both ideology and interest. Ideologically, the possibility that the imperialist states of Western Europe may transcend some of their contradictions is disquieting; and the traditional principles that underlie much of Soviet foreign policy indicate a preference for a divided Western Europe as being more amenable to Soviet interests than a united Community.

The Soviet reaction to proposals for enlarging the Community has not, on the face of it, been so consistent. In 1961-63 the Russians were in favour of British entry and now they are against it. But the inconsistency is only superficial. In 1961-63 the Russians expected that the enlargement of the Community would lead to its dilution, as well as to a weakening of what then seemed to them to be an anti-Soviet Franco-German axis. Now they do not expect the British to weaken the cohesion of the Community; and British policies are if anything less palatable than French and German ones.

The Russians have therefore refused to accord the Community legal recognition and have constantly denounced it as a discriminatory trading bloc, which should extend its internal tariff reductions to third countries. They have also tried to use their diplomatic influence to prevent British entry. Yet they have recognised the Community *de facto* on occasions when it suited their interests to do so, for example in signing international commodity agreements at the same time as the Community, and taking part in meetings of the Economic Commission for Europe in which Community representatives have participated and spoken. The Russians are, then, likely to accord recognition to the extent that they see a material interest in doing so.

Apart from direct economic advantages such as improved conditions of trade, it is entirely plausible that the Russians could come to see the uniting of Western Europe as serving the interest of high foreign policy by dividing the West, hitherto dominated by America, into two great blocs on either side of the Atlantic, which according to a traditional analysis might well come into conflict, and according to ideology would be bound to do so. These considerations lead one to expect that the Russians will not refuse to do business with the Community, and if necessary to grant it legal recognition, when they see some practical advantage in doing so.

East European governments have been more forthcoming in their attitudes towards the Community. Not only have most of them had numerous informal contacts with the Commission, but Hungary, Poland and Rumania have made formal agreements with the Community (those on sunflower seed oil, wines and turkeys, mentioned above), and Yugoslavia has formally recognised it. The East Europeans have a greater interest in trade with the Community than the Russians have. All of them send a higher proportion of their exports to the Community than the Soviet Union (in 1966, 8 per cent of Czechoslovakia's exports, about the same proportion of Bulgaria's, 11 per cent of Poland's, 13 per cent of Hungary's, 18 per cent of Rumania's and 28 per cent of Yugoslavia's, compared with 7 per cent of the USSR's); and in each case exports are a much larger proportion of total production. Exports of farm products are, moreover, particularly important to some of the East European countries, which are consequently concerned about the trade-restricting features of the CAP.

Politically, East Europeans have an interest in offsetting the Soviet Union's power over them by cultivating links with Western Europe. This has been explicitly done by Rumania and Yugoslavia, and Czechoslovakia was clearly travelling the same road when cut short by the Soviet invasion in 1968. That demonstrated to the other governments, if any demonstration were required, the need for caution in pursuing such a policy. The political as well as the economic logic of their situation nevertheless impels them to pursue it, and this, with varying degrees of enthusiasm, most of them do.

Integration in Comecon

It is often suggested that, in addition to their more direct reactions to the challenge of the Community, the Eastern governments have reacted by pursuing their own integration in Comecon.

The suggestion is not entirely unfounded. The establishment of Comecon by Stalin followed the launching of the Marshall-plan, and Kruschev's attempt to introduce supranational planning followed the establishment of the EEC. Although the organisation when Stalin set it up was little more than a name, and Kruschev's initiative foundered on the obdurate opposition of Rumania to any dilution of national sovereignty, there is still a great deal of talk about integration in Comecon and a substantial amount of economic co-operation does in fact take place.

There are significant forces that are conducive to integration. Thus the East Europeans increasingly feel the need for a larger market to give them the benefits of specialisation and large-scale production; and the Russians tend to want closer political control over the East Europeans, as witness their intervention in Czechoslovakia and its justification through the theory of limited sovereignty in the Socialist Commonwealth. But strong forces likewise work against it. The East Europeans on the whole resist closer control by the Russians, which would inevitably accompany integration with such a massive country; and the Soviet Union, although favouring the principle of economic integration, is big enough to lack much incentive for further economies of specialisation or scale.

More importantly, however, integration seems to go against the grain of the economic systems in Comecon. For the 'directive', or 'command', economy, depending for its operation on millions of instructions given by the planners to enterprises, can be integrated in any proper sense only by having supranational planners give millions of instructions – and, since the Russians would by their sheer weight inevitably dominate any supranational planning body, this means that each economy would be subject to very detailed Russian control. The Rumanians are not by any means alone in resisting that (even if the others are usually content to hide behind Rumanian resistance).

A further complication has been introduced by the more radical Hungarian reform to a 'guided market'[3] economy, in which many decisions on prices, investment and foreign trade are taken by the managers of enterprises, not by the planners. It follows that the Hungarians are beginning to face, in their relations with the directive economies that are maintained, even after reforms, by the other members of Comecon, many of the difficulties which have been found by Western market economies in their relations with the East, and which will be outlined below. While integration between a group of guided market economies would be much easier, because far fewer decisions would have to be taken supranationally, integration between directive and guided market economies would probably be still harder than the integration of directive economies alone.

What is called in the East integration is consequently not likely to amount to more than would, by Western definitions, be called co-operation, unless the Russians are moved for political reasons to force through a tough supranational planning organisation, or a sub-group of guided market economies in Eastern Europe were to integrate gradually without incurring a hostile Russian intervention. The former is not likely to happen unless the Russians believe, as they did in the case of Czechoslovakia, that countries are in the process of defecting from the bloc; and the latter will not happen until more East European countries have adopted a guided market system (only Hungary and Yugoslavia have yet done so) and unless they are so shrewd as to integrate at a pace slow enough and in a manner unspectacular enough for the Russians to accept.

PROBLEMS OF EAST-WEST ECONOMIC RELATIONS

The foremost fruit of a common external policy for the Community was fairly obvious from the start and was dramatically demonstrated by the Kennedy Round. Hitherto the United States had had no partner of comparable weight among the industrialised countries, and bargaining for tariff cuts in the GATT, based on the principle of reciprocal benefit, had therefore lost momentum. By confronting the Americans with a customs union of equivalent importance, the Community induced President Kennedy to initiate this major negotiation, and trade barriers were sharply reduced, not only for the two big partners but also for the other countries that were too small to have set such a process in train.

By analogy, the Soviet Union being so much bigger than any other European country, the Community might be expected to bring a better equilibrium into the relations between its members and the Russians, with a corresponding fall-out of benefits for the other European countries. Yet there is little evidence as yet of any idea as to how this might be done. Partly this is because Western Europe's trade with the East is small in comparison with trade with the United States and other industrialised countries. But a further reason is that tariff bargains count for little in East-West trade, and there is as yet no very clear conception of what might take their place at the centre of trade policy and negotiations between East and West. The economic systems prevalent on either side of Europe's great divide are so different that negotiations

43

have to deal with quite different problems; and these problems must be clarified before a valid policy can be proposed.

Before embarking on the analysis of these problems, it is necessary to qualify some simplifying assumptions on which such analysis is usually and conveniently based, and which should be somewhat modified because of certain changes that have occurred on either side. These assumptions are that the Western countries have market economies in which private ownership and free competition prevail, and the Eastern countries have command economies in which enterprises are state-owned and directed by the central authorities, and all foreign trade is conducted by state-trading monopolies. In fact Yugoslavia, and now – though to a lesser extent – Hungary, have given a substantial degree of autonomy to their enterprises and allow them to deal directly with firms in other countries; and the extent of oligopoly and of public purchasing and state ownership in the West is such as to raise many of the problems that the simplified model would attribute only to relations between East and West. Consequently Yugoslavia and to a lesser extent Hungary encounter problems in their trade with other Eastern countries similar to those that Western countries encounter; the relations between Yugoslavia, Hungary and the West are by the same token becoming relatively free of these problems; intra-West trade is not by any means immune to them; and the problems may be less acute in the relations between the East and the oligopolistic and public sectors in the Western economies than is the case with the more traditional private sector.

Despite these qualifications, however, the simplified model which is the basis of the following analysis demonstrates the problems that are still prevalent in East-West economic relations, with the virtually complete exception of Yugoslavia and the partial exception of Hungary, to which reference will therefore be frequently made.

Problems for market economies: unfairness

A frequent Western reaction to East-West trade is that the Western firm is dealing with a state-trading monopoly, that monopolies are prone to unfair trading practices, and that the treatment of the Western firm is therefore likely to be unfair. Yet in practice there are very few complaints of unfair treatment. Why this apparent paradox?

One reason is that most of the state-trading monopolies of the East European countries are quite small in relation to the size of the world market for the range of products in which they deal. Their share, and hence their capacity for applying monopolistic pressure in the world market for a given product, is often less than that of a big Western firm. The average Russian state-trading company is, however, much larger than the average East European one and hence more likely to be able to exert some market power at the world level.

There seems to be more scope for the exercise of bargaining power by the Russians, or the East Europeans, when they import than when they export, because they may place orders for large numbers of a given product or for large items, such as complete factories, either of which will be a very important transaction for the Western supplier. This gives the Eastern state-trading company a leverage that may be considerable. It can be exerted by imposing on the Western exporter onerous conditions of sale, and the suggestion has accordingly been made that a code of fair practices should be negotiated between Western and Eastern governments that would provide a framework within which any such abuses could be mitigated[4].

Where the state-trading company is using its power to exert leverage on price, however, a code of fair practice does not seem likely to help, and the remedies that have been put forward include the establishment (as in India) of state-trading companies in the market economies for the very purpose of conducting these negotiations, or the formation (as in France) of associations of firms interested in exporting a particular product to the East[5]. Such attempts to organise reciprocal monopoly power encounter the weakness that a Russian state-trading company may still be a large buyer of a product in relation to the whole export capacity, for that product, of a middle-sized Western country. If effective countervailing market power is to be instituted, the Community is in a better position to do it than the separate member states.

The unfair exploitation of Eastern buying power does not up to now seem to have caused great distress to Western firms, and action to counter it may therefore not be held to be urgent. The new enthusiasm for technical co-operation deals might, however, raise the problem more acutely; for the Russians have been promoting a number of projects each of which is worth many millions of dollars. The car factory being built by Fiat in the USSR is well known; the Japanese have undertaken the development of forest resources in Siberia and a major project relating to the construction of the Port of Vrangel; and major projects for a lorry plant, for the provision of irrigation equipment and for the development of Siberian mineral resources have been discussed with various possible Western partners. These projects are so vast, both operationally and financially, that the West European countries would seem fully justified in confronting the Russians with a consortium, including at least all those West European firms big enough to be the subject of a separate approach by the Russians. Such transactions are essentially of the kind where the strength of the whole Community is needed to counterbalance that of the Soviet Union; and the Community could use its power of control over external trade to ensure that the West European contribution in any such project was channeled through a consortium containing the relevant companies from the member states, which should where possible take the form of a European company, and which would negotiate and then direct the work.

When, however, one considers the disruption that might be caused by Eastern exports to the market economies, in the light of the differences between the two systems in pricing methods and economic structures, it is astonishing how little trouble there has been. Some cases have been recorded of the sale of commodities such as tin, cotton or aluminium at prices far below the world level, and other instances have been reported from time to time, but their number is remarkably small. The reason is that the policy of the state-trading companies is to sell at world market prices. Their motive is simple. They get more money on each sale than they would by selling below that price. They have doubtless had the experience of an anti-dumping duty imposed on goods sold more cheaply, and asked themselves why, if somebody is to collect a levy equal to the difference between the market price and any lower price at which the state-trading company might have been willing to sell, it should not be the authorities in the Eastern country rather than those in the West. They have been reinforced in this practice by a stipulation, inserted at the request of the British government in some of its bilateral trade agreements with Eastern countries, that exports to Britain under the agreement are not to be sold below local prices; (and the same applies, it will have been noted, to imports into the Community of sunflower seed oil, wines and turkeys from some East European countries). If the buyer is foolish enough to ask for a higher price, after all, why should the seller scruple to charge it?

One may well ask why a Western government should be so charitable as to ask an Eastern government to collect money which could be collected as taxation in the Western country, and take some of the burden off the local taxpayer, if the price is such as to justify the levying of an anti-dumping duty. The point is well taken; but there is a still more pertinent question to be asked. Does not much international trade take place because of differences in price? And if all differences in price are removed because the exporters always adjust prices to the level that prevails in the export market, won't a great deal of potential trade never take place?

The answer is not a simple one, because the prices in Eastern countries do not usually reflect costs as these would be understood in the West, so that a price difference does not necessarily signal that trade would lead to a better allocation of resources according to the criteria of a market economy. However, even after the complications of the differing price systems have been analysed, the answer remains, as we shall see in the next section, that much trade is lost, and that this appears to be a much more serious defect in the conduct of East-West trade than any unfair use of monopoly bargaining power.

The same may be said of the effect on trade of the obligation to deal with a state-trading company which is separate from the final buyer or seller in the Eastern country. This is an additional problem over and above that of dealing with a monopoly, which could (and in the case of a state enterprise in a Western country almost certainly would) be the final buyer or seller instead of an intermediary. The necessity of negotiating with such a middleman offers endless scope for misunderstanding and delay, which is not only frustrating for the Western businessman but doubtless also prevents some transactions from going through at all. In so far as exports from the East are frustrated by this, the level of trade in both directions is kept down, for any export earnings are spent by the Eastern countries on imports. The growth of Hungarian exports since the economic reform of 1968, which allowed producing enterprises a degree of direct access to export markets, indicates that a big potential export capacity may remain untapped unless Eastern countries reform their systems so that the middlemen – the state-trading companies – have a less dominant position.

Here, and repeatedly in the following text, we will see that certain reforms in the economic systems in Eastern countries would be helpful to economic relations with the West. Because the cold war has rendered these questions politically sensitive, and the Eastern authorities might react to pressure from the West for changes in their economic systems by a hardening of those systems and a deterioration of relations with the West, one feels a certain diffidence in putting forward such a conclusion. However, it is argued that such reforms would be equally conducive to economic efficiency and welfare in the East, and that they imply – as the reform in Hungary has shown – no change in fundamental political principles regarding the ownership of the means of production; and for these reasons the reforms in question are advocated by many economists in the East. It seems, in these circumstances, better to see where the economic analysis takes us, and rely on the responsible authorities to use any of the findings in ways that are politically and diplomatically realistic.

Misallocation

The fixing of prices and the taking of investment decisions are key determinants of the short-term and the long-term development of the economy. In the Eastern directive economy, the procedure for both is radically different from what is normal in the West, hence giving much scope both for complaints of unfair competition and for the misallocation of resources. As we have seen, the complaints of unfair competition are surprisingly few; but this probably reflects an even greater misallocation of resources than might be expected.

In the directive economy, the prices are fixed by the central planners. Since there are several millions of them to be fixed in each economy, the planners do not get round to fixing each one of them at sufficiently frequent intervals, and the price system is usually out of date in relation to the state of technology. The fixing of prices and incomes being done by the authorities, moreover, changes in them are a political decision of public moment, and some changes that could be economically justified (i.e. higher food prices in Poland so that farmers will produce more and will increase their very low incomes) are harder to make than they would be in an economy whose prices are more impersonally determined in the market. For these reasons prices in Eastern directive economies tend to be irrational by Western standards.

It is not certain whether this problem is inherent in the directive system or whether it can be removed by new techniques which the planners could employ for fixing prices. The Hungarians, in devising their New Economic Mechanism under which a large proportion of prices have been freed from central control, clearly believed that the directive system could not do the job properly. Others hope that a reformed and simplified directive system will be efficient enough in this respect, particularly as modern methods of data-processing come to be employed. However, the price systems in the directive economies are still generally irrational by almost any standards, and it will certainly be a long time before computers can remedy this – if they ever can –, so that problems of unfairness in East-West trade could be acute if the internal price level were not insulated from world prices by the state-trading companies, which are in effect applying taxes and subsidies to the goods traded in order to make up the difference.

Even if the planners in a directive system could find ways to fix prices exactly according to their intentions, there would still be problems in the relationship between Eastern and Western prices. For a long time the planners put no price on capital or land, so that capital-intensive or land-intensive products were under-priced by the standards of a market economy. With the reforms in directive systems, interest charges have been imposed, though almost always below Western market rates, so that the discrepancy has been reduced though not eliminated. According to market criteria, therefore, free trade would cause a flow of capital-intensive goods from East to West which would represent a misallocation of resources. Economic theory would therefore justify a compensating tax on capital-intensive imports from the East, and by the same token a subsidy on labour-intensive imports. Eastern planners do in fact themselves compensate, at least in part, by favouring the workers in 'heavy industry' (which is broadly the more capital intensive), thus giving them high wages and allocating lower incomes to those in light industry, services and agriculture. And in any case, whatever the rational price of the Eastern product would be according to market standards, the planners do not of course apply it in trade with the West, but effectively tax or subsidise their goods so as to sell at the 'world' prices, i.e. at prices fixed on the basis of Western factor costs. (The taxes/subsidies on goods sold internally in the directive economies have a quite different purpose, which is to make the capital goods cheap and the consumer goods dear to the final buyer, in order to maintain the very high rates of investment with as little inflation as possible.)

It follows from the practice of exporting at world market prices, regardless of the internal costs or prices of the goods, that the Eastern countries are failing to sell enough of the labour-intensive products in which they should have the comparative advantage, given the relative scarcity of capital in their economies when compared with those of the West. If it were not for the special characteristics of their internal and foreign trade pricing systems, Russia and Eastern Europe would have been selling to Western Europe large quantities of the labour-intensive manufactures such as textiles, clothing, footwear and light engineering products, which now come from half a dozen of the developing countries and from the countries of Southern Europe.

Lucky, perhaps, for the developing countries that Russia and Eastern Europe have not done so; but detrimental to the level of East-West trade and to the allocation of resources and the welfare of the people on both sides of the curtain.

The irrationality of the price systems, by the criteria of the market economies, is compounded by that of the investment decisions. Of course if prices are not a reliable guide to the relationship between supply and demand, they are not a good guide for investment decisions. But the investment strategy in the directive economies is determined not as a response to prices but by a political decision; and its central feature has been a concentration upon heavy industry – mainly metallurgy and capital equipment. During the course of successive economic reforms that have followed the death of Stalin, this concentration has become less extreme; but it is still pronounced in relation to what would seem to be the optimal strategy for a fast-growing market economy. This point, too, is confirmed by the Hungarians, who have further reduced the emphasis on heavy industry at the same time as introducing the guided market economy.

Thus even if the planners in the directive economies had been willing to sell their exports at 'rational' prices, they would still have been unable to supply the light manufactures in the amounts that importers in market economies would have demanded, because the goods were simply not being produced in sufficient quantity. In order to secure the most benefit for both sides from East-West trade, it would be necessary for the planners to invest more in the production of light manufactures. If the policy were extended so as to provide more consumer goods for the local populations as well, this would doubtless increase their welfare too, even after applying a suitable rate of discount as between present and future generations. (The workers in Poland have clearly been feeling this rather strongly.) But the minimum that is necessary, in order to optimise East-West trade, is enough investment to provide the quantities of these goods required for that trade. (This will not be sufficient, however, if a larger home market base is required in order to gain largescale, specialisation or external economies.)

This should not be taken as a root-and-branch criticism of the high-investment and heavy-industry strategy of the Eastern planners. Not enough is known of the causes of economic growth for us to condemn, on economic grounds, a method that has clearly achieved it. Such a method may well be better than leaving nature to take its course in the hope that individuals will take the initiatives and accumulate the capital required to pull an economy that is at a very low level up by its bootstraps. The supply of Puritans and Calvinists, who did this job in Europe, is not great in most of the less-developed countries, and many of them show every indication of remaining less-developed if nature is allowed to take its course. The question that needs to be asked is whether the New Puritans who hold power in the Soviet Union and Eastern Europe have not overdone this strategy. (Their own revisions of their policies show that they themselves believe this may have been the case.) And the firm hypothesis that is put forward is that East-West trade has suffered because the planners neither allocated enough resources for the production of light manufactures, nor priced their exports of such products so as to reflect their comparative advantage and thus increase their sales.

This, not unfair competition, is the main complaint that the West is entitled to level against the East. Both sides lose from the resulting misallocation of resources; but the East almost certainly loses much more. For their trade with Western Europe is a much higher proportion of their total trade and production than is the case reciprocally; and the Western countries can in any event obtain these products from a variety of low-income countries. (Of course the Western countries, because of a desire to safeguard particular interests and communities, or because of a generally protectionist philosophy, already deny themselves much of the benefit they should get from such trade, by imposing quotas and levying high effective tariffs on imports of labour-intensive products. But these restrictions are being relaxed, and do not in any case constitute a reason why the Eastern countries should not take advantage of the openings that are available. As we will see later, despite continued restrictions, these openings are now considerable.)

Relatively slight changes in the policies of planners in the directive economies – the allocation of more investment funds to the production of light manufactures for export and their pricing at levels somewhat below those of the world market – would cause a substantial improvement in East-West trade. These changes would be easy enough for the planners to make. But the change of pricing policy would encounter resistance in the West, because the more the trade is increased, the more complaints of unfair competition and of dumping there would be. Because of the irrationality of the pricing systems in the directive economies, moreover, the Western authorities would have no better basis for imposing anti-dumping duties than the fact that prices of the goods were below the local prices and injuring a local producer; and we would be back where we were before, with exports from the East priced at world market prices and trade that should take place being frustrated. Clearly under these circumstances the Eastern planners would not use such a pricing policy, because it would merely imply a transfer of revenue from their exchequers to those of the West. The hope that such trade could take place must wait, therefore, on Eastern countries adopting a guided market system with a price reform at least as radical as that of Hungary, if not of Yugoslavia; or on the directive economies adopting methods of price formation that are sufficiently rational and transparent to enable Western governments to make rational decisions about anti-dumping duties. For this reason, discussions about the methods and logic of price formation in East and West could be very productive for East-West trade in the longer run. The Economic Commission for Europe would be an appropriate organisation in which such discussions could take place.

Not enough trade: some further causes

The pricing systems, investment policies and trading institutions of the directive economies are such as may be expected to cause, as we saw in the previous section, not only a misallocation of resources and hence a distortion (by almost any standards according to which these things are judged in the market economies) of the pattern of East-West trade, but also the frustration of a large volume of trade which would take place, to the benefit of both sides, but for these organisational obstacles.

The alignment of the exports from Eastern countries on world market prices, their concentration on the development of heavy industry at the expense of light manufactures, and the inhibiting complexity of their system of importing and exporting exclusively through state trading monopolies all give reason to suspect that East-West trade is far below the optimum level. This suspicion is confirmed by the figures, which show such trade to be well below the prewar percentage of the European countries' total trade. There are, moreover, other weighty causes that contribute to this result.

Bilateralism

The bilateral balancing of trade is well known to be prominent among them. A market economy usually has surpluses with some of its trading partners and deficits with others, with the sum of the surpluses balan-

52

cing (apart from any persistent capital flows) the sum of the deficits, when one year is taken with another. Without the 'triangular' trade that is represented by these bilateral imbalances, the total trade would be greatly reduced – precisely, indeed, by the sum total of the bilateral imbalances. But the elimination of these useful imbalances is exactly what the planners in the directive economies set out to do. They have a general preconception that trade with each trading partner should be balanced; and the trade statistics confirm that they generally succeed in this aim. The trade in each direction between an Eastern country and a Western trading partner is usually at a remarkably similar level. This is not, as is sometimes believed, because payments are made in bilateral blocked accounts which must be clared from time to time. The bulk of payments are made in Western currencies which the authorities in the Eastern country could use in their trade with other countries, if they so wished. Nor is it for any other reason that is inherent in the nature of the directive economy. This is shown by the fact that the Soviet Union runs a surplus of about £ 100 million a year with Britain, the earnings from which the Russian authorities use to buy commodities from overseas sterling area countries. Clearly the Russian planners find it convenient to organise their bilateral balancing with the sterling area as a whole instead of with its several member countries such as Britain or Malaysia – although there is nothing inherent in the sterling area as a monetary system which should lead them to treat it in this way, sinces sterling is a convertible currency. It would be equally logical, from this standpoint, for the Russians to regard all the countries of the West as belonging to a single IMF currency area, and to balance bilaterally, not with individual Western countries, but with the West as a whole – or more precisely to the point in the context of this particular paper, with the European Community as a whole instead of with the individual member states, as should indeed be done if the common commercial policy towards the East is to be introduced in 1973.

This treatment of the sterling area as a unit shows, indeed, that bilateral balancing with each country is not inherent in the external trade system of a directive economy. If they come to regard a particular area as the unit with which a balance must be struck, they can quite well strike that balance, allowing surpluses and deficits with individual countries within the area to cancel each other out. Conceptually, there is no reason why this unit should not comprise the whole convertible currency area of the world. The practical difficulties for the planners are not such as might at first sight be expected, and such as did, clearly, lead the Russian planners who developed the system to believe that a simple bilateral balance was required. For an examination of international trade statistics shows that the surplus or deficit between a pair of countries is often quite stable from year to year, so that the planners, once having discovered (as the Russians did with the sterling area) where their 'natural' bilateral imbalances lie, could build these imbalances into their trade plans. Annual fluctuations could be dealt with, as they are now, by means of credit balances; and changes believed to be secular could be built into successive trade plans.

Unfortunately, once the directive economies have introduced the system of bilateral balancing, we find resistances in the West against its removal, on the grounds that multilateral dealings would be unfair, given the special characteristics of the Eastern system. The parallel is striking with our earlier observation that an apparently simple change in Eastern pricing policies to reflect the Eastern countries' comparative advantage would not by itself be practicable because Western countries, confronted by more competition from an economic system which has a method of price formation that appears to be irrational, would cry dumping and enforce the restoration of the trade-frustrating practice of alignment on world market prices. The resistance to multilateral trade comes from the Western countries that would have deficits with Eastern countries. Clearly, if the Eastern countries are to have deficits with some market economies they must (assuming for the moment that an Eastern country cannot pay for a deficit with the whole group of market economies with the earnings from a surplus earned within the Eastern bloc) have surpluses with others. But a surplus for an Eastern country is a deficit for its market-economy trading partner; and once the authorities in the market economies have got into their heads the idea of a trade agreement that provides for bilaterally balanced trade, it seems hard to get them to accept the idea of negotiating for a bilateral deficit. This is understandable enough in the case of countries suffering from chronic global deficits which they find it hard to rectify. But some of the countries that resist a bilateral deficit with the East have strong balances of payments, and those that do not would in most cases do better to resolve their difficulties by global measures such as adjustment of the exchange rate, rather than by detailed distortions of the pattern of trade. The Western countries that might have to accept a deficit do, however, have a good argument on their side. This is that they are being asked to make their currency convertible for the Eastern country to spend where it wants, but that the Eastern country will not respond by making *its* currency convertible should the balance of trade change and the Western country earn a surplus. In so far as bilateral imbalances are likely to be long-standing, because they result from structural factors in the international economy, this argument is not valid. It is also subject to a criticism similar to that which is levelled against protection by the proponents of unilateral free trade. But by the same token, and by analogy with the argument for reciprocal tariff reductions such as result from negotiations in the GATT, even if the market economies would be better off by allowing multilateral trade of the type represented by a triangle with one apex in the East and two in the West, they would be still better off if the Eastern countries would make a concession in exchange – for example by allowing multilateral trade represented by a triangle with one apex in the West and two in the East, and eventually allowing Eastern currencies to be converted into Western currencies. According to this argument, the use of convertibility of Western currencies to multilateralise East-West trade should be accompanied by the convertibility of Eastern currencies earned in such trade, or by some equivalent concession on the part of the East.

Such policies have been proposed by the Hungarians since the introduction of their guided market economy in 1968. But convertibility presents great difficulties for the directive economies as they stand at present – though it will be argued below that these difficulties are not inherent in the system. Indeed, limited convertibility arrangements have been made in trade agreements between certain Eastern countries and developing countries such as India and Brazil, which enable each of the later to conduct triangular trade within Eastern Europe. But the obstacle which stands in the way of such agreements with Western countries is that the Western currencies are hard and the Eastern ones are soft: that is to say, given the existing relationships between prices and exchange rates in Eastern and Western economies, it is not likely that any Eastern country would exchange its earnings of a Western currency for another Eastern currency. If this is so, convertibility would not result in any transactions; and if this is expected to be so, convertibility would be embarrassing and will not be allowed.

The Eastern countries already have experience of a convertible rouble which can be used for settlements within the Comecon. But this has not been used as widely as might have been expected, and this is a poor augury for convertibility of one Eastern country's Western currency earnings into another Eastern currency, given the much greater price/

exchange rate disparity between the two blocs than exists within them.

If the difficulty lies in disparate relationships between exchange rates and the levels of external trade prices in East and West, then it could be remedied by changing the exchange rates. For the directive economies, with the insulation of their internal prices from their external trade prices, this is purely a bookkeeping operation; and it seems a pity that a book-keeping change should stand in the way of a major step towards multilateral trade. If there were signs that Eastern countries would be ready to make substantial moves to convertibility, as the Hungarians have suggested, and so translate this monetary reform into real terms by a corresponding move towards the multilateralisation of their external trade plans (setting off surpluses with some trading partners against deficits with others so as to reach a global balance), then it would be well worthwhile for the Western countries to guarantee the Eastern ones against the risk of an unexpected global deficit, by offering a substantial amount of credit. Just as multilateralism was introduced in Western Europe after the war through the European Payments Union, set up with the help of an American loan, so Western Europe could help Eastern Europe towards multilateralism with the help of a loan for an East European Payments Union – or, indeed, for a European Payments Union extending to the whole of Europe.

Lack of investment-type transactions

Private investment in industry is of course anathema to Marxist-Leninist ideology, and it has long seemed pointless to consider the contribution which it might make to economic relations with the Soviet Union and Eastern Europe. But the Yugoslavs since their 1965 reforms have allowed foreign firms to have, under certain conditions, a minority holding in Yugoslav enterprises; and in the Comecon countries arrangements described as technical co-operation, some of which have several of the attributes of direct investment have become increasingly common.

It is by now fairly well known that international investment is becoming a more important element in the world economy than international trade, and that much trade takes place as a result of such investment, and even as between a branch of an international firm in one country and another branch of the same firm in another country. All this activity reflects economic advantages to be gained from the transfer of finance, technology and management or specialist skills. In the West, these transfers often take the form of investment, in which they are accompanied by elements of ownership and control. This is often the most advantageous form of transfer for the investing firm, and hence maximises the volume of such transfers; but at the same time ownership may carry with it problems of sovereignty and independence for the country receiving the investment. The Eastern countries' ideology renders them exceptionally sensitive on this issue of ownership, so that the transfers of finance, technology and skills have to take place without that framework of fully-fledged investment which is a central feature of so many such transfers within the West. Hence the many and complicated forms of 'technological co-operation' with Western firms that have recently sprouted in the East; but hence also, because such agreements will frequently appear less advantageous to the Western firms than simple direct investment, a reason for the lower level of such transfers from West to East than might be expected if one considers their tremendous expansion within the West.

The desire on both sides to benefit from such transfers is such as to evoke a great deal of ingenuity in devising forms of agreement which will give the transferring firm as much as possible of the control, security and profit that it wants without transgressing the ban on private ownership of industrial capital. The Yugoslavs have, as we saw, found their solution in the limitation of ownership by foreign firms to less than one half share in a Yugoslav enterprise. The Hungarians, for their part, have devised an arrangement whereby an American hotel company has managerial control and what amounts to a fifty per cent equity in a hotel in Budapest for a period of fifty years. This almost leads one to ask whether this confrontation between the thesis of private ownership and the antithesis of public ownership is leading to a synthesis of private ownership (with public participation) for a fixed and limited period of time. And it certainly raises the question whether carefully worked-out forms of co-operative arrangements, which are being pioneered by some firms working together with the appropriate organisations in the East, might not, as and when they prove successful in practice, be used as the bases for a series of framework agreements which would be officially agreed by the authorities on both sides to be fair from both points of view and recommended for use by enterprises.

Since the granting of credits and the development of technology are undertaken by the public as well as the private sector in Western countries, the transfer of finance and technology may be directly negotiated between Eastern and Western governments; and here again is a field of policy which may be quite as important in East-West relations as tariffs.

Inadequate marketing

Practical businessmen often suggest that lack of skill in marketing is the main reason why Eastern exports to the West do not rise faster, and that this is therefore the chief constraint on East-West trade in both directions, since imports into the Eastern countries are limited solely by their earnings of foreign exchange. An economist's reaction to this may be that failure to sell will be due to a combination of factors such as quality, delivery dates and price as well as marketing skills, and that if you think that exports are too low you should recommend a cut in the exchange rate. In this way you can arrive at a price which will attract the buyer, after the other factors have been taken into account.

But it is well known that, whereas economists may be clever, businessmen are sensible, and we should not be too surprised if there is something in what they say. What they have done, after all, when they make such a comment, is to compare the performance of Eastern producers and exporters with the standards to which they are accustomed, and to find that marketing is the area in which the East is relatively weakest; and this conclusion is consistent with what theory would lead one to expect. For the central feature of the directive economy is that the managers of enterprises respond to instructions from planners, not to signals from the market; and it is therefore natural that they should be less attuned to the consumer's needs, and hence less apt to produce and sell in a way that is most likely to lead the consumer to buy.

Those responsible for exporting from some Eastern countries have sought advice and training in marketing skills; and some of the more far-sighted among Western business people who are interested in exporting to the East, realising that such exports will rise only if the East earns more by selling to the West, have been trying to encourage this development. Doubtless this will do some good, and the state trading companies responsible for exports will improve their techniques. But proper marketing depends on an approach that is orientated towards the needs of the consumer, in the methods not only of selling but also of production; and it is hard to see this approach percolating through the producing enterprises as well as the trading companies in economies where the focus is towards, not the point of view of the consumer, but the commands of the planner. Thus it may be that the directive economy is inherently deficient in marketing, and that the only means of radical improvement within the present Comecon system is a reform to the guided market economy.

Problems for Eastern economies: Western trade restrictions

When confronted with all these suggestions that East-West trade would be bigger and better if the directive economies made this or that reform in their systems, a natural Eastern reaction would be that the West should put its own house in order, and change those Western practices that stand in the way of trade. The target is usually Western restrictions on imports from the East.

With respect to tariffs, the complaint is usually about those cases where most-favoured-nation treatment is not accorded to Eastern countries. Under United States legislation, MFN treatment is given only to Poland and Yugoslavia, though West European countries give such treatment more generally. As long as the Soviet Union refuses to recognise the European Community, however, the Community will clearly have good reason not to give the Russians MFN treatment, which following the completion of the Kennedy Round cuts would imply a relatively low tariff level. Quotas are a more widely spread constraint and, although in the last five years many have been swept away, most Western countries still keep a hard core on agricultural products and 'sensitive' manufactures such as textiles. Eastern countries have reason to fear that, with British entry into the EEC, their agricultural exports will come up against more restrictive barriers than before.

It was argued earlier that it would be logical for Western countries to remove their quotas from imports from the guided market economies, in so far as the latter introduce methods of price formation that are sufficiently rational by the standards of Western market economies. As regards imports from directive economies, it would seem legitimate to bargain quota removal against changes that would improve the Eastern systems from the point of view of East-West trade.

An implication of this is that only guided market economies should be eligible for treatment as full members of the GATT, with quota restrictions against them removed. For these countries, indeed, tariffs and tariff cuts can have some meaning. The Polish guarantee, on the other hand, made on Poland's accession to the GATT, that its imports from member countries would rise by 7 per cent a year, does not seem to be a very appropriate concession. The rate of growth can be achieved only if Poland's exports rise at the same rate, so that the imports can be paid for; and who is to say that, given Poland's existing directive system, this is more suitable than a lower rate of growth? Doubtless it is useful for countries with directive economies to participate in the GATT organisation, so that mutual trading problems can be discussed and agreements can be sought as to what constitutes good behaviour as between countries with such different economic systems. But although, for political reasons, this may be called full membership of the GATT, it should be seen as a special kind of membership; or, more fruitfully, the GATT may be developing into a house with a number of rooms, one of which would be the room containing industrialised market economies, with the fairly rigorous trading rules that are appropriate to them, while another would contain the directive economies.

Unreliability of Western markets for Eastern exporters

When producing for the home market or for export to another directive economy, the enterprise in a directive economy is instructed by the planners how much to deliver in a given plan year and has the certainty that when the goods are delivered they will be taken up. When the planners conclude a trade agreement with a market economy, however, they have no guarantee that the goods agreed to be exported to the market economy will in fact be bought. It all depends on whether the importers, who are quite separate from the government signing the agreement, want to buy them or not. So planners sometimes complain that this unreliability of market economies is a great drawback to doing business with them.

In practice, the exports of Eastern countries to the West seem to be fairly stable from year to year; and this stability should be reinforced by two factors: any improvements in marketing which the directive economies may achieve (even against the grain of their systems); and the conclusion of medium-term contracts with big firms in the West, such as a recent agreement whereby components for motor manufacture are imported by Renault from Rumania. The latter factor is, indeed, an interesting example of the way in which big firms introduce planning concepts and methods into their own operations within the market economies; and it may not be so surprising that this is some help to trade with directive economies, which are based entirely on plans for deliveries over the medium term.

Once again, for the exporters of Hungary and Yugoslavia since their reforms, the nature of market economies does not constitute a special problem, because they face the need to find markets and make sales within their own economies too. The more that Eastern countries adopt such reforms, the more smoothly East-West trade will be conducted, from the point of view of East as well as West. But although the problems that the Eastern directive economies encounter in their relations with Western economies are doubtless annoying for them, those problems that arise as a result of actions by the West, with a few exceptions such as agricultural protection, do not seem to be severe. The reason is fairly simple. The Western countries have never really known how best to react to the trading methods with which the East has confronted them: state-trading monopolies, bilateral balancing and inconvertibility. The trade has been undertaken largely on the terms of the directive economies of the East, which have therefore naturally managed to avoid any great difficulties. In the following, and final, section we will consider how the largest trading group among the market economies – an enlarged European Community – might work out a policy for East-West economic relations that would satisfy its own political and economic interests as well as those of its trading partners in the East.

THE EUROPEAN COMMUNITY'S INTERESTS AND POLICIES

This paper started by noting the disparity between the greatness of the political importance of the relations between Western Europe and the East and the slightness of the Community's policies towards Eastern Europe and the Soviet Union. The import quotas on steel and the agreements about the prices of sunflower seed oil, wines and turkeys are, indeed, no more than responses to the Community's internal market problems, and are not intended to achieve any other objective in relations with the East; and, while the Commission is justly quite proud of its long 'liberalisation lists' of products on which the member countries have all agreed not to impose quotas on imports from Eastern countries, the member countries were anyway in the process of rapid liberalisation and the basic aim of having Community lists was not so much the wide one of achieving a substantial improvement in the conditions under which East-West trade takes place (which was certainly a main objective of the national programmes of liberalisation), but the narrow one of attempting to ensure that no *détournements* of trade take place because of different quota arrangements in the different member states. In initiating the common liberalisation lists, the Commission was doubtless using the Community's well established vendetta against distortions of competition partly in order to achieve a wider political and economic aim by presenting it as a legal and technical device. But one suspects that a major motive was also the pursuit of uniformity as an end in itself; for if a wider policy towards the East is a more important aim, the right strategy would be to implement a significant first instalment of liberalisation, in order to demonstrate goodwill and the capacity for action beneficial to the East, and then to make it clear that further liberalisation lists would be forthcoming for Eastern countries which would negotiate about them. As will be argued below, there are extremely important subjects on which it would be desirable to negotiate with Eastern countries; and, although the Community has or could develop a number of economic instruments with which to negotiate, it seems a pity to throw away, by massive unilateral action on common lists of liberalisation, one of the major ones that exists at present.

The chief economic instruments of which the Community disposes at present for bargaining with the East are the common external tariff (both MFN and non-MFN), import quotas, and import policy relating to agriculture. In addition the Community, despite the unhappy experience of Euratom, has, and will doubtless develop much further, a capacity to negotiate about technological co-operation. When a European company law has been established, the Community could, as has been hinted earlier, use this in order to match monopoly power in the East, and particularly the Soviet Union; and meanwhile big European companies could be encouraged to form consortia for the purpose. It is already conceivable that the European Investment Bank could make loans for projects of interest to the East, for example East-West transport links; and the Community could certainly create new capacity to offer credits in connection with the transactions of Community firms with Eastern countries.

At the level of institutions, the Community will have the power to conduct negotiations with the Eastern countries after 1 January 1973, and this should extend to the negotiation of the bilateral trade agreements which at present constitute the framework for most East-West trade. The Community should have a policy regarding the participation

62

of Eastern countries in international organisations and the development within those organisations of a framework for East-West relations, and, given the Community's importance in the organisations, such a policy would carry great weight.

Finally, it may be worthwhile to observe that the Protocol relating to German Internal Trade and Connected Problems would have to be renegotiated should the DDR ever be recognised by the Community's members as a state in international law. Since the DDR's exports enter the Federal Republic duty-free under this protocol, and since this trade is estimated to be equivalent in value to the whole of the Community's trade with other Eastern countries, it is evident that there would be something to negotiate about that is of very great interest to East Germany.

Having listed all these instruments, which could give the Community very considerable scope to pursue an effective policy towards the East, let us now see what the aims of such a policy might be.

Policy aims: preventing unfairness

If unfair competition is narrowly (and often unfairly!) conceived as meaning the sale of goods at lower prices than those that prevail on the local market, then it is not much of a problem in East-West trade. Existing anti-dumping legislation is all that is required to deal with it; and the Community merely needs to add the right of appeal to a Community authority if one member country claims that its market is being disrupted because of inadequate anti-dumping action by another. This problem will become difficult only as and when Eastern countries reform their pricing systems radically (as the Hungarians appear to have done), so that people in the Community can accept that when an Eastern product is cheaper it has some genuine comparative advantage; and when they furthermore cease (as it is not yet clear whether the Hungarians will do) the general practice of aligning their exports on Western prices.

The main problem of unfairness is, as was argued above, not the type that is called 'dumping', but other methods of exploiting the market power of the really big state-trading companies, and hence particularly those in the Soviet Union. By negotiating bilateral agreements for the whole Community, by ensuring that major co-operation projects are undertaken by a consortium of firms from the member countries or where possible by a European company, and by disposing of a capacity to grant credits and offer technological co-operation at the Community level, the Community institutions can introduce the countervailing power without which the separate countries of Western Europe would, because of their smaller size, remain at a disadvantage in dealing with the Russians. This, like the EEC's participation in the Kennedy Round, is an economic aspect of the political argument for enabling the European Community to countervail, at least to some degree, the superpowers.

The other side of this coin is that an enlarged Community would be much larger, in relation to the several East European countries, than the Soviet Union is in relation to the larger among the West European states. One might wish that the East Europeans would respond to this by establishing their own East European Community, but such a hope is politically unrealistic at present. The Community therefore should, for political as much as economic reasons, be very careful not to abuse its power in its relations with the countries of Eastern Europe. The focus of the common policy, as far as establishing equality of bargaining power is concerned, should be the Soviet Union. Apart from this, there is (except in so far as the Eastern countries introduce guided market economies and change their export pricing practices) little need for common action to prevent unfairness to groups or member countries in the Community. There is, as emerged from our earlier analysis, much greater scope in the objective of the expansion of trade.

Policy aims: expanding trade

There is no doubt that a significant growth of East-West trade would follow from the removal of quotas on the import into the Community of agricultural products and 'sensitive' manufactures. The increase of Eastern countries' exports would be followed immediately by the spending of their foreign exchange earnings on imports from the market economies. The definitive fixing of the Community's tariffs on imports from the East at MFN levels could also provide some incentive for greater trade. The question remains, however, as to whether the Community should promote such trade expansion with the East unconditionally, or whether some conditions should be attached to what amount to important concessions. The answer depends, surely, on whether the Community has interests that could both fairly and realistically be expressed in the form of such conditions.

One such interest was discussed in the preceding section: the use of

64

bargaining power to countervail the size and strength of the Soviet Union. For this to happen, the Soviet Union must recognise the Community to the extent of negotiating bilateral trade agreements with it. The Community should certainly be cautious about making concessions to the Soviet Union, whether of MFN tariff levels or of quota liberalisation, before such recognition has taken place. Beyond this simple point regarding bargaining power, however, the conclusion of the earlier analysis of problems of East-West economic relations is that a market economy such as the Community does have legitimate interests to safeguard or promote, and that these concern more than anything else the methods by which Eastern countries organise their pricing, investment and trade.

First, it is clear that the market system in Yugoslavia and the guided market system in Hungary are removing or alleviating many of the difficulties that have arisen in trade between market economies and directive economies. It is entirely legitimate, for this reason which is rooted in economic fact and not political value-judgement, that the Community should offer these countries, and any others which introduce similar systems, access comparable to that enjoyed by trading partners from among the market economies, to the full extent that a given guided market economy organises its production, pricing and foreign trade in ways similar to those practised by market economies. Not to do so would truly constitute unjust discrimination against countries such as Yugoslavia or Hungary.

Secondly, there are changes that the directive economies can make in their systems of external trade which would make it easier for market economies to envisage a greater growth of trade, as well as enabling the directive economies to improve their own trade performance. These changes – which have already been introduced to some degree by some directive economies – would include a relaxation of the monopoly of state-trading companies, so as to allow direct transactions between Western firms and producers or buyers in the Eastern countries; a more rational and transparent method of price formation, at least as far as exports are concerned; a higher priority for those industries in which the Eastern countries enjoy a comparative advantage; and at least a degree of multilateralisation of trade and payments. It is suggested that the degree to which the Community encourages and liberalises trade with a given Eastern country should depend on the extent to which that country has introduced such changes, and is willing to discuss with the Community the remaining problems and their possible solutions. There would, then, be a spectrum of liberalisation and of financial and technological co-operation on the part of the Community, depending not on purely political criteria such as attitudes of independence from Russia (that is another matter), but on the economic criterion of the ease with which the Eastern country's system allows trade to be conducted and expanded with the Community.

If the Eastern countries continue their trend of recent years towards reform of the directive systems and even the introduction of guided market systems, and if the Community responds by enhanced liberalisation and co-operation to each step taken in the East, the expansion of trade could be quite dramatic; and this would fully justify not only the internal adjustments in agriculture and some other industries that liberalization would imply and technological co-operation (e.g. credits, support for an East European Payments Union, and joint projects of technological development). But it must be recognised that the strictly economic interest of the Community as a whole in such trade is rather limited, because the growth of trade will remain a small part of the growth of total trade, and its income effect (and hence welfare effect) will be a very small proportion of national incomes, in countries where the welfare benefits from further growth of incomes may be subject to rather sharply diminishing returns. The economic benefits would accrue, rather, to particular export industries in the Community, and generally to the East because of the greater importance of relations with the Community in their trade and in their total production, and because their incomes are still lower so that additions to those incomes are more desirable.

Policy aims: political

Even if the economic interest for the Community in greater East-West trade is not very great, however, the political interest is quite another matter. The political value of trade which takes place very much at arms' length between mutually inconsistent and perhaps hostile systems may be questionable; but there can be little doubt of the value of a process of harmonisation or of reaching agreement regarding fair conditions of mutual transactions, or of the human relationships that are central to many of the types of co-operation agreements now being developed. (One is very conscious, in raising this subject in a conference organised by scholars from Leyden, that this is not the first time

66

that the idea of convergence has been given both a political and an economic meaning. But one may also hope that Leyden people will be satisfied that ideas which germinated here have taken root and flourished in so many other places.)

Hopes that good may come of such a trend are surely not too unrealistic. But it is as well, in a world still dominated by the presence of the nation-state, to have at the same time one's feet on the ground where foreign policy has stood for many centuries. On this ground, it is axiomatic that the preponderant weight of the Soviet Union is bad for Europe, and that a better balance between the Soviet Union and a united Western Europe should be secured if it can be. A European Community with a clear and effective external economic policy towards the East would be a very important step towards such a balance.

While a basic aim of the European Community should certainly be to safeguard itself, by common action, against damage due to the disproportionate size of the USSR in relation to any of the Community's member countries acting separately, the Community's weight should also be used, as far as is reasonable and practical, to alleviate the extent to which East European countries live in the shadow of the Soviet Union. The very existence of such a large trading partner would offer East European countries at least a certain counterweight to the abuse, from their point of view, of Russia's economic power. It should, indeed, better enable them to avoid being induced against their will into a process of supranational economic integration with the Soviet Union, which would be against both their interests and those of Western Europe (and, because of national backlash in Eastern Europe, in the long run against the interests of the Russians too). By the same token, an effective Community policy could help any such group of East European countries towards a similar process of integration among themselves, which would be as beneficial, politically, as supranational integration with Russia would be detrimental.

This brings us back to the perspective of a Community whose external policies might, while not ignoring those traditional concepts of foreign policy which are imposed by the nature of the existing international system, at the same time transcend those concepts and work for the creation of a new and better system. To encourage the establishment of an integrated community in Eastern Europe would be one example. An increasingly co-operative relationship between the European Community, the United States, the Soviet Union and any community that may grow up in Eastern Europe would be another. This depends, in part, on a continued process of convergence between the economic and social systems in East and West, and it would be necessary for the Community's policy-makers to be well aware of any such trends and alive to the possibilities they may open up for closer East-West relations. It might, indeed, be hoped that the Community will, as it evolves, develop policies which provide convincing answers to some of the criticisms that are levelled by socialists against the system of ownership of the means of production and the distribution of wealth that prevail in the West, and which seem to many people in Western countries to have some foundation. In this way, if reforms continue in the East, convergence could increasingly be seen as a reality. At the same time, one can envisage a more co-operative relationship being developed with other parts of the world, thus forming a network which would become the basis of a world community.

Are such thoughts no more than social science fiction? It is amazing how many of the imaginings of the early writers of science fiction have now been translated into reality. Without some sense of historic direction, there is no chance of breaking out of the *status quo* where officials of national trade and finance ministries haggle about petty commercial advantage (and where Community officials spend too much time worrying about petty distortions of trade). With such a sense of direction, there is at least a chance that the Community could play a part in the delivery of a more humane world system.

NOTES

1. Eastern Europe is defined here as Albania, Bulgaria, Czechoslovakia, the DDR, Hungary, Poland, Rumania and Yugoslavia. 'The East' is used (with apologies to China, India, Indonesia, Japan *et al*) to refer to Eastern Europe and the Soviet Union together.
2. The Community had of course explicitly renounced any intervention in the relations between East and West Germany, in the Protocol to the Treaty of Rome, relating to 'German Internal Trade and Connected Problems'.
3. The term is taken from Kaser, M. and Zielinski, J., *Planning in East Europe,* The Bodley Head, London, 1970.
4. Samuel Pisar, *Coexistence and Commerce,* McGraw Hill, New York, 1970, Chapter 25.
5. *Loc. cit.,* pp. 478, 479.

East-West relations in Europe: institutional aspects*

J. KAUFMANN

* The views expressed by Mr. Kaufmann, who is at present Ambassador and Permanent Representative of the Netherlands to the Organization for Economic Co-operation and Development, Paris, are strictly personal and therefore do not necessarily reflect those of the Netherlands Government.

1. INTRODUCTORY REMARKS

To outsiders the notion East-West as used to connote a real or imagined economic-political borderline in Europe cannot fail to make an odd impression. Turkey at the geographical Eastern end of Europe and Greece at the very South are counted as being part of Western Europe; Poland is considered 'Eastern Europe', Finland at the North end 'Western Europe'. Of course, all this can only be understood as part of history, in particular developments after the Second World War. The Cold War, which in economic terms can be considered to have started in 1948 when the Soviet Union, followed by its allies, rejected the Marshall Plan, provoked a distinct split in economic relations. The Economic Commission for Europe, soon after its establishment, became divided in two blocs[1]. The Council for Mutual Economic Assistance, in spite of obvious differences, became the Eastern pendant for the OEEC. After an early postwar start with the Benelux economic and customs union, in Western Europe the movement toward economic integration advanced in successive rapid steps, such as the Schuman Plan, the Rome Treaty. This is not the place to engage in a full comparison of various institutions. They can, as a test of the 'profoundness' of international co-operation, be analysed as to the degree of international and supranational guidance accepted by participating member countries. Developments in East-West institutional relations can thus be looked at in terms of (a) broadening the number and scope of international East-West agreements and (b) increased transfer of powers to international or supra-national organs.

In economic terms it would seem plausible that the more the economic systems and methods of operations in Eastern and Western countries become alike, the easier it would seem to have common institutions. We shall therefore start with a brief discussion of the so-called convergence theories, and then discuss certain specific aspects of East-West relations.

2. IS THERE CONVERGENCE OF EASTERN AND WESTERN EUROPEAN ECONOMIC SYSTEMS?

Ever since Tinbergen wrote his famous article in 1961[2] replying positively to the question whether Communist and Free economies show a converging pattern, a lively discussion has occupied many pages of economic and other journals. It has become clear that convergence

71

means different things to different people. We shall leave aside, for purposes of this article, political convergence.

Of course, political détente, and thereby implicitly, political convergence, is an almost indispensable prerequisite for convergence in any economic matters. Real convergence defined not only as increasing similarity in statistical phenomena, but a common understanding on the functioning of the economy, requires a climate of confidence or at least of decreasing lack of confidence. Therefore an understanding on major political issues dividing Eastern and Western Europe will provide the setting for further progress in economic convergence. At the same time it can be argued that economic cooperation will promote political détente.

For convenience sake we subdivide economic convergence in:
a. technological convergence (of production processes)
b. convergence of economic structures, organisation, and policy
c. convergence in patterns of accepting supra-national control or guidance.

a. *Technological convergence*

Obviously, the requirements of modern industrial society imply that East and West endeavour to apply modern techniques. Convergence in this sense, real as it may be, is not typical for East-West relationships, since even as far as developing countries are concerned, modern technology imposes its specific requirements, Technology is a great 'converger' everywhere!

b. *Convergence of economic structure, organisation and policy*

The ECE Secretariat has summarized as follows its comparative study of the structure of manufacturing industry in Western and Eastern Europe (ECOSOC doc. E/5007, based on the Economic Survey of Europe in 1970)

'(a) Structural shifts (particularly the increasing shares of engineering and chemicals and the declining shares of textiles, food processing and fuel have narrowed the differences between country patterns and have tended towards convergence on a common pattern of output by branches.

(b) The branches with the fastest productivity gains are not necessarily the same in different countries. Chemicals generally show the fastest increases and food processing among the slowest. But while, for example, engineering mostly shows fast increases in Eastern Europe, it does not always do so in the West, and while the textiles industry shows relatively slow productivity growth in the East, its performance is not far from average in the West.

(c) Foreign trade appears to reflect a high degree of mutual trade and specialization within branches, particularly for metals, engineering and chemicals (and, in the West, textiles)'.

Some insight into the degree of convergence is provided by the trends in the distribution of output between major branches of economic activity. The following table (nr. 1) on the distribution of output between major branches of manufacturing may be of some use:

Table 1. Distribution of output between major branches of manufacturing (unweighted averages for each group)

	Eastern Europe and Soviet Union		Western Europe		Convergence or Divergence
	1950-52	1966-68	1958-60	1964-66	
Metalmaking	10	10	7	6	—
Engineering- and metal products	17	30	27	30	+
Chemicals and rubber	5	9	11	11	+
Wood, paper and products	8	6	14	14	—
Textiles, clothing leather	21	14	17	16	+
Food, drink and tobacco	33	21	17	15	+
	6	10	7	8	—
	100	100	100	100	

Source: data derived from provisional version of Economic Survey of Europe, 1970.

This table shows some convergence in as much as the sector 'engineering and metal products' has shown an increase for both Eastern and Western Europe, but more so for Eastern Europe, probably because its capital goods industry was relatively underdeveloped. Generally the structure of Eastern European industry has moved in the direction of that of Western Europe. However, the movement is not uniform. This is visible in the last column of table 1 showing convergence or divergence, depending on whether the spread between the percentage shares of Western- and Eastern Europe has decreased or increased in comparing the two periods listed.

Table 2 summarizes the development of trade within each region:

Table 2. Percentage shares by sector of intra-trade for:

	Eastern Europe 1957	Eastern Europe 1967	Western Europe 1957	Western Europe 1967	Convergence or Divergence
Foodstuffs, materials and fuel	46	29	36	25	+
Machinery and transport equipment	27	37	22	29	—
Other manufactures including 'miscellaneous' goods	27	34	42	46	+
	100	100	100	100	

Source: Economic Commission for Europe, *Analytical Report on the State of Intra-European Trade,* United Nations, New York/Geneva, 1970, page 103, table 10.

For what may be considered the most dynamic sector, that of machinery and transport equipment, the relative movement has been non-converging. This is confirmed by a comparison of mutual trade in the capital goods sector: West European exports to Eastern Europe of machinery and transport equipment have risen (as a percentage of total exports to Eastern Europe) between 1957 and 1969 from 24 to 40%, while similar Eastern European exports to Western Europe stayed stationary at 10% for the same period.

The Economic Commission for Europe summarized its findings on industrial organization in the following terms:

d. 'Small establishments (plants) of less than 100 workers account for 40 to 50 per cent of total employment in manufacturing in most, but not all, Western European industrial countries; in the less industrialized, the proportion is generally still greater. But the proportions in small *enterprises* tend to be appreciably smaller. In most of Eastern Europe, large enterprises (over 1,000) account for the biggest share of employment and large establishments also seem to be more important than in the West.

e. An analysis of output (value added) per worker in Western Europe indicates that productivity most often increases with the size of establishment up to a certain point, but there is a levelling off thereafter. In Eastern European countries productivity (in terms of gross output) also tends to increase with the size of the enterprise.

f. In Western Europe, the merger movements and the rationalization of industrial structures have continued to progress and have been favoured by governmental policies, although efforts also continue to discourage monopoly and restrictive business practices. There has also been a trend in Western Europe towards increased foreign participation in manufacturing. In Eastern Europe governmental policies have tended in varying degree to enlarge the area of enterprise autonomy; at the

74

same time there has been a general tendency towards the grouping of enterprises under large management and supervisory units representing approaches towards a 'multi-level' system of managements'.[3]

Unfortunately, the available material does not permit direct comparisons. Presumably, the conclusion is justified that the gradually increasing autonomy at the enterprise level in Eastern Europe signals a convergence with the situations in Western Europe.

c. *Convergence in patterns of accepting supranational control or guidance*

The question is inevitable whether real convergence of economic systems is possible, in the longer term, without some common understanding on the acceptance of international or supranational guidance and – sometimes – control.

With the accession of the United Kingdom, Denmark, Norway and Ireland to the European Economic Community the Western European integration movement is receiving a new impetus. Economic policies in the broadest sense will be co-ordinated through Community organs.

There is also co-ordination through the Organization for Economic Co-operation and Development. On the side of the Eastern European socialist countries the Council for Mutual Economic Assistance has shown less far going efforts towards economic co-ordination of the participating countries. The Economic Commission for Europe has summarized these as follows:

'Various efforts have been made during the postwar period to achieve economic integration within CMEA. The main instruments used were the co-ordination of plans, long-term trade agreements, and other centrally determined measures of bilateral co-operation between governments. While these measures have been successful up to a point, a stage in the development of the centrally planned economies has been reached where new measures to achieve a higher degree of integration of the CMEA area are deemed necessary. This is the main purpose of the comprehensive programme of further intensification and improvement of co-operation and development of socialist economic integration of CMEA member countries adopted at the 25th session of the CMEA in Bucharest, July 1971.'[4]

Such are the centripetal forces of Western European economic integration that unless there is a similar movement on the Eastern side, the convergence of certain economic and statistical data is bound to be overshadowed by the differences in acceptance of supranational guidance and control. One will find that Western countries will, whether they like it or not, increasingly accept common standards and guides

75

on various matters. Co-ordination with the Eastern countries will be difficult, unless common organs on that side are able to negotiate with European Economic Community organs. The Economic Commission for Europe could be available as a point of contact and mutual co-ordination.

3. WIDENING AND DEEPENING EAST-WEST CO-OPERATION

It is undoubtedly the merit of the Economic Commission for Europe to have – throughout its 25-year existence – provoked a substantive number of agreements between East and West, in spite of numerous technical, political and psychological difficulties. Few of these East-West agreements and arrangements contain real supranational elements. With some effort one can detect slight supranational elements in some arrangements, namely in those cases where the Secretariat, in casu the ECE Secretariat, has the task to report on the implementation of some agreement or arrangement.

The Conventions, Agreements or Protocols concluded under the auspices of the Economic Commission for Europe (up to and including 1971) can be summarized as follows.

on Agriculture: Geneva protocol on Standardization of Fruit and Vegetables, adopted in October 1954, revised in 1958.

This Protocol has formed the basis for a series of European standards which as of October 1971 covered 40 fruits and vegetables.

on Trade: European Convention on International Commercial Arbitration, signed at Geneva on 21 April 1961, entered into force on 7 January 1964.

on Inland Transport: On road traffic 11 conventions were concluded, of which those on road signs and signals are no doubt best known. The Agreement Concerning the Adoption of Uniform Conditions of Approval and Reciprocal Recognition of Approval for Motor Vehicle Equipment and Parts (of 1958, modified in 1967) has led to a large number (25 as of March 1972) of regulations.

on Inland Waterways: Three Conventions.

on Customs Administration: Nine conventions, of which the best known is the so-called TIR Convention facilitating the international transport of goods by trucks.

on Transport of Dangerous and Perishable Goods: Three conventions.

It is symptomatic for the state of affairs as it has existed throughout these postwar years that few East-West agreements on trade have emerged. One cannot say that there has only been a 'dialogue of the deaf', since numerous meetings under the auspices of the Economic Commission for Europe have certainly led to a clarification of positions of the market economy countries of Western Europe on the one hand and the socialist countries of Eastern Europe on the other hand. These positions have continued to be divided by a profound abyss: the Western European countries are not willing to commit themselves to abolish all remaining quantitative restrictions and controls; as is persistently requested by the Eastern European countries. The Eastern European countries do not want to commit themselves, in spite of systems of government purchasing, to purchase increased quantities of goods in the Western European countries. Yet there has been progress outside the Economic Commission for Europe. The accession of Poland to GATT is governed by a protocol under which in exchange for a general promise (without specific date) to abolish quantitative restrictions, Poland accepts to increase its annual imports from other GATT countries (taken together) by a certain percentage (namely 7%)[5]. The accessions of Hungary and Rumania (not yet successfully completed) to GATT may show a similar pattern of mutual undertakings. In this way there is some progress in what may be called the semi-multilateral field: the relations between one socialist country and a group of market economy countries. Similarly, there exists of course a large and growing network of East-West bilateral trade agreements. But evidently, there are fundamental difficulties for both sides to engage in far-going multilateral commitments on trade relations.

Work continues under ECE auspices on certain practical aspects of East-West trade. As Mr J. Stanovnik, Executive Secretary of the Economic Commission for Europe, noted in a statement to the UN Economic and Social Council (July 7, 1971):

'Expanded work was undertaken in regard to the simplification of trade procedures ... we are still today operating with trade procedures, documents and the handling of exports and imports, with the methods which have been largely devised in the nineteenth century ... In ECE we have now begun the work of developing a code language for the foreign trade documents which would be fed directly into computers and would thus make foreign trade procedures as simplified as those of internal trade ... We have also undertaken another rather important work on standardisation, as analysis has shown that a great hidden obstacle in East-West trade was the fact that different standards are applied and that therefore the importers have been hesitant in purchasing products produced on the basis of different standards and which might require a great deal of adaptation and additional cost. We are also organising a special seminar on marketing, on business contacts. We are undertaking another rather interesting feasibility study on the possible establishment of a center for industrial co-operation. One of the ideas being exposed is the possibility that such a center might bring together for industrial co-operation enterprises in one country with unused capacity and enterprises in another with insufficient capacity'.

Technological exchanges and industrial co-operation have all become intermixed with trade in the narrow sense. It may well be that pragmatic solutions on the practical problems involved in this wider concept of East-West trade are more important traditionally conceived undertakings on most-favoured nation treatment, abolishment of quantitative restrictions or market access. When the time is ripe, perhaps after greater general détente and successful experience with the pragmatic solutions I have just referred to, more far-going legal undertakings will become possible without stranding on the present obstacle of fears of certain economic consequences and mutual lack of confidence. On industrial co-operation increasing numbers of intergovernmental East-West agreements are being concluded. Apparently they do not meet with the same difficulties as trade agreements often do. They are of course mostly 'accords de cadre', setting the general framework within which specific deals must be consummated between individual enterprises or for specific transactions.

As an institution, the Economic Commission for Europe could well assist these developments by the adoption of common standards, guidelines or agreements. The Commission is also considering the establishment of a Centre for Industrial Co-operation which would undertake a clearinghouse function in relation to specific transactions. Something similar might be considered for technological co-operation in general, if this would meet clearly noticeable needs. Especially, the environmental field, where numerous problems present common characteristics all over Europe, offers a fruitful area for joint investigation and action.

4. SHOULD NEW EAST-WEST INSTITUTIONAL MACHINERY FOR ECONOMIC MATTERS BE ESTABLISHED?

This question should be answered in the negative. Present institutions are capable of absorbing current economic issues for the purpose of international discussion and the setting of standards or conclusion of agreements. The central body for this should remain the Economic Commission for Europe, whose cumulative experience, both in the secretariat and as a deliberative body, is most valuable.[6]

Are there other organizations with a potential or actual role in East-West relations? OECD and CMEA are not particularly suitable for engaging in East-West arrangements, because each is geared to the particular problems of a more or less homogeneous group of countries with common characteristics. On the other hand each of these organizations may be in a position to supply the 'raw materials' on which ECE could 'build' for certain East-West arrangements of agreements. Also, EEC and CMEA might use ECE as a common framework for exploring certain questions.

While this central role for ECE appears logical, it can be argued with almost equal logic that nothing should prevent GATT from providing a framework for contractual East-West trade relations. However, efforts to 'multilateralize' such understandings as are included in the Poland-GATT protocol of accession run into the sort of difficulties sketched above. Perhaps, later, a new chapter of GATT could be written on the way trade negotiations between state trading and market economies are to be conducted (as we endeavoured in the original Havana Charter). By that time, however, trade relations in the narrow sense are likely to have been superseded by economic relations of a more encompassing nature, including industrial and environmental co-operation.

The Council of Europe is now limited to Western countries. It is conceivable that some day it will include Eastern European countries among its members. It is inconceivable, however, that at such time it would start duplicating economic work which is already undertaken in ECE and elsewhere.

Finally, a word on the European Security Conference. There are several differing formulas how it is to function and which fields it should cover. Presumably, the ESC will wish to discuss economic matters. It would, however, be a mistake to set up new permanent machinery for the follow-up of any economic discussions. A link should be established as early as possible with the Economic Commission for Europe, and its secretariat, so that the latter can act as the executive arm for whatever economic work the ESC may agree upon.

NOTES

1. On developments in the Economic Commission for Europe see Jan Siotis, 'ECE in the Emerging European System', *International Conciliation,* January 1967.
2. J. Tinbergen, 'Do Communist and Free Economies Show a Converging Pattern?', in *Soviet Studies,* April 1961, pp. 333-341. The literature on convergence is analysed and a full bibliography provided, in J. van den Doel, *Konvergentie en*

Evolutie, Assen 1971. (*Convergence and Evolution,* with a summary in English).
3. Also from doc. E/5007. For a full discussion see Economic Commission for Europe, *Economic Survey of Europe in 1970,* Geneva/New York, 1971.
4. Economic Commission for Europe, *Economic Bulletin for Europe,* Vol. 23, no. 2, november 1971.
5. Cf. Bohdan Laczkowski, 'Poland's Accession to GATT', *Journal of World Trade Law,* Vol. 5, no. 1, January/February 1971. See also Frans A. M. Alting von Geusau (editor), *Economic Relations after the Kennedy Round,* Leyden, A. W. Sijthoff, 1969, Chapter III, Zdenek Augenthaler, 'The Socialist Countries and GATT', Chapter IV, Bohdan Laczkowski, 'Poland's Participation in the Kennedy Round', Chapter V, Johan Kaufmann and Frans A. M. Alting von Geusau, 'The institutional framework for international trade relations'.
6. On the role of international secretariats generally, see Johan Kaufmann, *Conference Diplomacy,* Leyden/New York, Sijthoff and Oceana, 1968, Chapter VI.

The European Community and the neutrals

A. MOZER

Twenty years after the splitting up of Western Europe, under substantially changed political circumstances, efforts are being made to overcome that split; the slogan being 'Enlargement of the European Community'. At the time (in 1950), the French government under Robert Schuman proposed to all member countries of the Council of Europe the creation of a functional community, i.e., the Coal and Steel Community. The negotiations were to be attended only by those countries that were prepared to meet one condition: to transfer a part of the national power of control over the basic industries coal and steel to a High Authority, a communal organisation. Only six members of the Council of Europe, actually the six first members of the European Community, were willing to embark on this adventure. I may assume that you are familiar with the further historical developments, the abortive defence community and the political community linked with it, up to the establishment of the European Economic Community and its development to date.

Seven of the West European countries not involved in this experiment established the European Free Trade Association (EFTA), proceeding from the assumption that suitable co-operation suffices for this form of association, whereby the customs barriers between the member states of the EFTA are abolished, but the sovereign right to charge national external tariffs is respected.

Meanwhile three of these EFTA countries and Ireland are involved in the negotiations for the enlargement of the European Economic Community. This is a renewed effort, the first attempt at British membership in 1963 having been thwarted by the French veto, a veto of which MacMillan said: it came because the negotiations threatencd to succeed . . .

Three of the member countries of EFTA (Sweden, Switzerland and Austria) and one country closely linked with EFTA (Finland) are now negotiating individually with the EEC concerning their relationship with the EEC.

In the case of these 'Neutrals' (to give a rough and ready definition of the special status of the countries in question) their position in international politics constitutes a problem in their relations with the EEC.

This status of neutrality, whatever it is based on, precludes membership. The EEC has transcended the limits of the customs union and is on the way to economic and currency union. Whatever the number and duration of the stages in which this goal is achieved, the fundamental decision has been made, and this political decision by its very nature rules out membership of these countries. Whereas in conversation with nationals of these countries one can enter into political philosophies about the relevance of national independence today, the decision rests with these countries themselves and commands respect.

However, that does not end the discussion. For the next question is what forms of closer relations – taking into account the political decision of these countries – are to be found, which will satisfy the wishes and the needs of both parties. To accuse the EEC of 'excluding' a number of countries which in their social structure belong to Western Europe, would be too easy a way out. Just as it goes without saying that the autonomous decision of these countries must be respected, so there is justification for the attitude of the EEC in refusing to subordinate the Community's structure to this decision.

In the quest for forms of relations that can be reconciled with the views of both parties, the concept of association is often put forward in debates. The former Chairman of the EEC Commission, Prof. Walter Hallstein, undoubtedly encouraged these debates with his statement that the scope of association ranged from 1 to 100, from trade agreement to near membership. In discussions with the neutral countries of Europe this leads to misunderstanding.

In EEC practice – since the association of 18 African countries and Malagasy, the association of Greece and Turkey – association means a stepping stone to membership; an expedient, because the economic development of the associated countries does not permit of the immediate reciprocity of the rights and obligations. Obligations, possibly related to customs policy, which the Community undertakes, need only be undertaken in stages and after prolonged intervals by the associated countries. These unilateral performances of the EEC result from the view that these developing associated countries must be allowed a period of adaptation before they have to meet the same conditions as the highly industrialised countries. This concession does, however, also entail institutional disadvantages for the countries in question. During the association phase they do not take part in the decisions of the organs of the Community. The mechanism of a council (Community – associated country) built into the association agreement is merely the institutional means of applying EEC resolutions already adopted to the association relationship.

From this basic definition of the term association it follows that association is unacceptable for the countries considered here. No one would dare to suggest that Switzerland, Sweden or Austria come within the range of the developing countries. To grant them unilateral preferences would not be justifiable. At the same time, however, these countries, which have no voice in the decision-making process of the EEC, can hardly be expected subsequently to have to accept these resolutions within the framework of the association. For the neutral countries the association procedure followed up till now would mean in practice the surrender of more of their independence than would full membership, which would give them a consultative voice and right of co-determination.

In so far as association is discussed in the aforementioned countries, it is a result of confusion concerning the essence of the concept association. In Vienna, Stockholm, Bern and Helsinki I have repeatedly tried to make this point clear, and sometimes I noticed signs of regret, sometimes a sense of relief . . . In any case, I am convinced that it is the decision of these countries themselves that makes association in the traditional sense pointless in these cases.

So long as the practice of the EEC was limited to the phase of the customs union, the obvious solution to strive for was that of the free trade area, as a link with these neutral countries. In accordance with the nature of the free trade area, the neutral countries would agree to mutual demolition of tariffs, but vis-à-vis third countries they would retain own tariff walls. Any resulting deflection of the flow of trade would then have to be corrected with the system of certificates of origin, as it is in EFTA. As for the possibility of such a solution, Finland's relationship to the EFTA could serve as an institutional example, for that country is associated with the EFTA, yet at the same time forms a free trade area with the USSR.

Considerations of this kind have become more academic, now that the EEC is widening its scope beyond the limits of the customs union, not only by agreement, but also in practical ways. It may be assumed that the Community would reject the solution of the free trade area with the neutrals on grounds connected with the shift in the flows of trade. These difficulties should, of course, not be exaggerated, especially when one considers the effective weight of the customs tariffs in relation to the inter-governmental manipulations in the field of trade obstacles. Here, we are, however, entering upon the working sphere of the economic union, which the neutrals refuse to take over, because of the consequences of an internal European policy for national sovereignty.

If we invoke both the economic and the political argument that also with these countries mutually desirable relations should be established, the only possibility left open is the preferential trade agreement. Here, of course, objections are raised by third countries, on commercial as well as on political grounds. Whereas association aimed at subsequent membership can be reconciled with the rules of the GATT, this is much more difficult in the case of a preferential trade agreement. In addition there is purely political resistance. Regardless of the contrasts between the US State Department and the Department of Trade, viz., that the State Department weighs commercial drawbacks against the political advantages of European union, to which it definitely attaches importance, this political advantage is lost in the case of purely commercial preference.

There the point is reached where one has to abandon the summary notion of neutrals and turn to a differentiated view of the position of these countries whose neutrality varies considerably. The collective term no longer suffices for the individual countries.

Only Switzerland has the status of neutrality in the traditional sense. I think it extremely unlikely that she is prepared to relinquish this status. Her industrial interest in a link with the Community is obvious. Her agrarian interest to a much lesser extent. True, the Swiss are interested in exporting agrarian produce, but their own agricultural policy – in which the subsidies far exceed the level of the Community's – is based on self-sufficiency in the event of war. From the point of view of currency Switzerland has no need for unification. The fruitless discussions between the German Minister of Finance Möller and his Swiss partner – talks between federals and confederates – on tax oases and hot money has demonstrated this. And yet, politics is the decisive factor. Currently efforts are being made to submit all agreements entered into by the Swiss government to a national referendum. Alfred Zehnder, for many years Switzerland's ambassador in Moscow, an opponent of this referendum on State agreements, recently effectively outlined the desirable policy for Switzerland. Whilst he does not dispute the interdependence of the world, he does believe that Switzerland should seek and recognise this interdependence 'where it is politically least harmful for Switzerland'. That leads him to the following political maxim:

'It is essential that every citizen should know what he wishes for Switzerland. If it is independence and emphasis on national sovereignty, he must strive for membership of the United Nations Organisation. If Europe is what he wants, then he must be prepared to sacrifice autonomy. If, on the other hand, he wants a stronghold against the modern world, then he will op for the referendum on State agreements'.

Hence, there is no denying that in the latest discussions within Switzerland the neutrality concept is being formulated anew. However, this is by no means a question of abandoning the existing standpoint, but merely one of more flexible interpretations, which allow a little more elbow room at the political level in a world whose independence has meanwhile been discovered by the Swiss as well. At any rate, things are reported which in the past would have been unthinkable. I would recall the latest, indignant reaction of Switzerland to a substantial reduction in the contribution Austria is prepared to make towards its defence. The Swiss Government expressed its concern that Austria was capable for reasons of internal policy to devote so little attention to its own security; the very security of a country with which Switzerland has a common frontier. This is an eloquent example of the appreciation of the interdependence of the world, that they worry about disarmament, but not about the rearmament in the neighbouring country. In the face of this conflict (which has meanwhile been settled) where the concern did not arise from fear *of* Austria but anxiety *about* Austria (and, consequently, about Switzerland), a historical reminiscence can hardly be suppressed. Switzerland owes its neutrality to the quite touching agreement between three of its neighbours to begrudge each one of them Switzerland. Meanwhile, in the minds and attitudes of the Swiss this neutrality has become a national achievement. Those neighbours who used to be rivals because of Switzerland, are now joined together in a European Community . . .

For the process whereby Switzerland must make up its political mind, it is necessary to compare two considerations that motivate the advocates and the opponents of an agreement linking Switzerland with the Community. The opponents do not entirely dismiss the theory of the continuing process of interdependence, but want Switzerland to practise extreme moderation. They are guided by past experience, when every delay, whether it concerned the League of Nations or the Council of

Europe, gave Switzerland advantages as regards the form of the link. The advocates, on the other hand, maintain that these comparisons are defective, for with the EEC it is a case of a steadily strengthening process of cohesion, which constantly increases the distance to the outsiders.

In the customary discussions Sweden's status is usually equated to Switzerland's. This is a mistake. The aim of Sweden's foreign policy is to have no foreign policy. Though Sweden definitely claims the right to take a stand on foreign policy, she pursues an autonomous policy, without ties to any bloc, including a link with the unaligned countries whose leaders include, for instance, Tito.

The error of this equation is clearly illustrated by the controversy between the Netherlands Foreign Minister Luns and his Swedish colleague Torsten Nilsson on the occasion of the former's visit to Helsinki early in November 1970. In an interview on Swedish television he expressed his doubt about Swedish neutrality. On the following day Torsten Nilsson, also on Swedish television, reacted rather sourly. He thought that Luns with his views was isolated, for other countries knew very well that Sweden pursued a foreign policy which, though not neutral, was independent. He pointed to the support the Swedish delegates on the Council of Europe were lending to the Dutch efforts directed against the Greek Junta regime. He thought that Luns' criticism stemmed from his disappointment at the fact that on the Vietnam issue Swedish foreign policy had led to standpoints that were at variance with the Dutch. Lastly, in response to Luns' advice that Sweden ought to associate with the EEC, Nilsson pointed out that, after all, institutionally association could only be considered for developing countries ...

Sweden's foreign policy, essentially realistic and at the same time independent of ties, has its roots in the recent past. In two world wars Sweden succeeded in remaining neutral. They attribute this not to decisions reached in the capitals of the belligerent countries, but to their own decision. At the end of the second world war, during initial discussions in Stockholm I was to hear: 'You' (the Dutch) 'should have followed our example in remaining neutral'. I endeavoured to make it clear that it had not been ourselves but Berlin that had made the move ... The line of thought followed by my Swedish discussion partner was that Göbbels had been right after all in alleging that Holland had attacked the Third Reich. At the time of the Hague Conference in 1948 and Churchill's appeal for a United Europe, the then Swedish Prime Minister Tage Erlander said to me, and these are his actual words: 'In two world wars we managed to keep out of the firing line, do you now want me to go to my country and try to sell them the idea that we definitely want to be in on it next time?'.

Naturally, one feels the need to spare oneself the reproach of lacking world-wide solidarity. They make a substantial contribution towards development aid. Names like Dag Hammarskjöld, Gunnar Jarring or Mrs. Myrdal, the Swedish delegate to the Geneva Disarmament Conference, show the direction in which Swedish foreign policy wants to make its mark. Far less convincing is the allusion to the services Sweden's autonomous attitude renders its Scandinavian neighbours – notably Finland, but also Norway. In Oslo and Helsinki the verdict on this performance is far less positive than they would like you to believe in Stockholm.

Especially from the industrial side Sweden's entry into the EEC has been advocated for years. In order to avoid conflict within the Nordic countries, but also to make people aware of Sweden's isolation, the campaign has often been conducted under the slogan 'Scandinavia must join the EEC'. Meanwhile the Swedish Parliament has decided that no effort shall be made at membership. The present minority government of the Social Democrats under Olof Palme needs toleration on the part of the Communists. Without sufficient backing from his own party, the youthful and intelligent Prime Minister could not take the risk of a coalition with a bourgeois party. His position as the spokesman of modern radicalism, which compels him as the party and government leader to make compromises, makes him feel uncertain, especially since he lacks the toughness essential in such a situation.

We may expect that in questions of world politics Sweden will make its voice heard, but is disinclined to show any involvedness in European problems. In a different context, viz., with Finland, some observations remain to be made concerning that country's efforts to turn Sweden's attitude to its own advantage.

Austria's attitude is predictable. It is not my own interpretation, but that of the former Foreign Minister and present Federal Chancellor Bruno Kreisky, that Austria owes its International Treaty and, with it, the withdrawal of the occupying powers to her policy of patiently awaiting developments and then seizing the opportunity that presented itself. This applies to the situation that had arisen in the early 'fifties, when the discussions on the European Defence Community were being conducted. The International Treaty with Austria was no doubt dangled before Western German's nose as a bait, to show what she might be offered by way of a peace treaty, should she refuse to join the EEC. Up to the very last minute Vienna was uncertain of the outcome. When the Austrian delegation alighted from their plane in Moscow, and a Russian military band played the new Austrian national anthem, Kreisky was heard to say: 'They want to come to terms with us, or they would not have practised this anthem . . .' Austria is committed to neutrality 'after the example of Switzerland', as it says in the agreement. People in Austria are very touchy if one suggests that neutrality did not stem from their own decision, but was imposed upon them by a foreign power. Strictly speaking that is not true, either: Austria had the choice of getting rid of the occupying powers on these terms, or not. They made their own decision.

My first talks with the then Foreign Minister Kreisky about joining the EEC date back to 1958. The EEC existed on paper. Hardly anyone had taken cognizance of it. It would have been grateful for every expression of sympathy, any feeling of solidarity. Kreisky showed me his estimate of the foreign trade Austria would lose if it did not join the EEC, and how he proposed to make up for these losses: in the EFTA, in Asia. At the time there was no question of worrying about a Russian Veto. In fact, Moscow had not even bothered to take any notice of the EEC. What worried Kreisky, and continued to determine his attitude in the years that followed, was the fear that a link with the EEC, whatever its form, might be or become a repetition of Austria's 'Anschluss' with Germany.

In the latter years of the coalition governments under Gorbach and Klaus the problems of integration were withdrawn from the Foreign Ministry and consequently from Kreisky's influence and entrusted to the Ministry of Commerce. This made no difference to Kreisky's decisive influence. True, the representatives of the Austrian People's Party made numerous attempts to strengthen the relations. Each demonstrative speech was followed by a call on the Government in Vienna from Moscow's representative, who had meanwhile become very alert. The eagerness for integration vanished just as quickly and enduringly as it had started. A special part was played for a while by the then Minister of Agriculture, Dr. Schleinzer, who advocated association, not because he did not realise the institutional consequences, but because he cherished the hope that the obligation to adopt the EEC resolutions in the agricultural sector would make this agrarian policy easier for him vis-à-vis an Austrian Parliament which was not prepared to take these steps on its own initiative.

In the 'sixties Kreisky was an advocate of building a bridge between EEC and EFTA. Disappointment at the lack of solidarity on the part of the British with the EFTA partners then induced him to enter into negatiations with the EEC without awaiting the decisions of other EFTA countries. The almost ten-year-old talks between Austria and the EEC have at times experienced the effect of the South Tyrolean negotiations. Strangely enough, little leaked out about the extent to which Gaullist France played a part, which with increasing reservation watched the steady strengthening of Western Germany, and then saw the closer relations with Austria, again from the angle of the undesirable 'Anschluss'. By contrast, the question of South Tyrol did not seem to be the real reason for Italy's disinterested attitude towards Austria as much as that country's interest in Yugoslavia, with which it established increasingly close economic contacts in an attempt to equate the closer relations between the EEC and Austria to its own overtures towards Yugoslavia.

Today the preferential trade agreement seems to be the only possibility Austria is prepared to discuss. Fear of an indirect 'Anschluss' has strengthened; not only in the East. Just as much in the West, especially since the West German diplomats have been so eager to become the mouthpieces of Austrian interests in the Community, regardless of the desire for reticence the Austrians had frequently intimated to them.

Somehow or other Austrian politics still evoke the old witticism: The state of the world is serious, but not hopeless; in Austria the position is hopeless, but not serious. Anyone who recalls the restrictions in regard to armaments imposed on Austria under a treaty, and who watches an Austrian military parade, can only wonder at the lack of expert knowledge of American or Russian military attachés, when they see that it includes weapons of far larger calibre than Austria is supposed to possess. Actually, these are old stocks of weapons which were supplied to Austria by the signatories of the treaty . . .

Let me conclude with some observations about Finland. This country's dependence on the Soviet Union is on the whole more evident than Austria's. The latest instance, which seems to strengthen this view, is the unexpected refusal to join a Nordic Community, which already seemed perfect. In Helsinki it is pointed out that the real reason for Finland's withdrawal was the almost simultaneous declaration by the Nordic countries that they now wanted to enter into negotiations with the EEC. Finland's Foreign Minister Väino Leskinen justifies this action on the grounds that, in contrast with Austria, he does not permit situations to arise which will clearly lead to intervention by Moscow, but that instead he realises what degree of latitude he has and then decides accordingly. Leskinen is a man from the Tanner group, one of the dedicated social democrats during the Finnish-Russian war. The mere fact that Leskinen, who for many years was persona non grata in Moscow, was able to become Foreign Minister and is now considered to be in Brezhnev's confidence, is quite remarkable. He himself has justified it towards me with the simple observation: 'We have to live'. The country has 2,000 kilometres of common frontier with Russia. The obligation to pay reparations has lent Finnish industry a structure which makes it largely dependent on east-oriented trade. Leskinen who with his realignment has subscribed to President Kekkonen's policy, justifies all this on the grounds that in Moscow the strives for the maximum (economic) elbow room for Finland, and in doing so meets with understanding. At the same time this rules out any agreement with the EEC which covers more than trade policy. In the course of talks I had with him he expressed the hope that consideration for Finland, so often promised by Sweden, would now at long last be honoured, by Sweden limiting itself to a trade agreement with the EEC and managing to evolve a common formula for Sweden and Finland.

One of the countries in the borderland between East and West is undoubtedly Yugoslavia. This is the only country that has freed itself from the Soviet embrace, regardless of its internal political structure. The prerequisite for this lay in the fact that Yugoslavia owed its liberation not to Russia's armed forces, but to its own national achievement. Together with Nasser, Tito worked his way to the top of the non-aligned countries, the remarkable thing being that whereas Tito moved farther away from Moscow, Nasser moved nearer to it. Towards the end of Nasser's life relations between the two leaders were slightly strained, for the very reason that Tito reproached Nasser for being too uncritical in his approach to Moscow. The conversation between Tito and Nixon on the day of Nasser's funeral took the form of a serious warning by Tito against Soviet-Russian lust for expansion. Tito considers himself not only the representative of the non-aligned, but also thinks of himself as being a politician without illusions. From West

European countries he expects economic and military aid, without such aid having to be demonstratively proclaimed.

It may be useful to draw a number of final conclusions. With all the differentiation between the positions of what are called the neutral countries, the obvious need for the EEC, especially after its enlargement, is that it should be aware of the legitimate wishes of these countries and act accordingly. This will scarcely amount to more than trade concessions, and even these should not be capable of being politically misconstrued.

On the political level a worthwhile contribution from these countries to the East-West relations in Europe is hardly to be expected. In the mutual relations between the EEC and these countries the maintenance of a 'cordon sanitaire' between the blocs is certainly not unimportant. The zeal with which, for instance, Austria and Finland compete to be the location of conferences – SALT, European Security Conference – is aimed more at their own security as a meeting point than at involvement. This zeal is concerned with the interest the countries of the Eastern bloc are taking in the European security conference, hoping from such a conference that it will loosen their shackles formed by the bloc and by the Brezhnev doctrine. The chances of these conferences being a success are rated more pessimistically the nearer one gets to the Soviet frontier.

Quite a different conclusion could be drawn from this European situation if the members of the EEC, enlarged in the future – it is hoped – by the present candidates, could decide on a common trade policy and with it a common foreign policy. Doubtless the Government of any one of these countries gives the assurance that it is concerned with nothing but aims. The practical reality, however, looks different. What we are experiencing is the heyday of the bilateralism of the West European vis-à-vis the East European countries. If the EEC countries and the differentiated neutral countries are allowed to go on gravitating towards the East in the present manner this will further the foreign-economic and the foreign-political disintegration process, without resulting in the slightest parallel development in the Eastern bloc. It affords one bloc under the sign of the Brezhnev doctrine the opportunity, exploited to the full, to play the Western countries off against each other. This applies not only to their trade relations, where the practice of outdoing each other in the size, the terms and the duration of credits is in full swing. On the other hand, it makes no contribution whatsoever to the one thing the West professes it wants above all: a process of development which lessens the ideological contrasts and their effects on practical politics. Our instinct for self preservation should prevent us from surrendering ourselves to this game of playing off one country against another.

The complete removal of tension, another avowed aim, also necessitates such a policy. For a detente can only be achieved if one is prepared to accept certain established facts as they are. One of these established facts is the existence of a closed bloc under the hegemony of Moscow. Any attempt at bilateral influencing will end in the same way as it did in Czechoslovakia. The West should abandon not only the hope of a break-out, but also refrain from any action that might provide an excuse for such events.

Instead, a policy directed at easing the tension should move in the direction of economic discussions, with EEC and Comecon seated opposite each other as partners. Only in this confrontation, which brings decisionmaking bodies face to face, is a process of relative emancipation within the Comecon possible, after the example of the EEC. This is also the only way in which it is possible without danger to loosen the shackles imposed on the Comecon countries under the hegemony of Moscow. Anyone familiar with the common trade policy in the EEC knows just how far removed we are from this integration phase. Even so, one can expect more from it than from the role of the neutrals.

Summary of the discussions

Several speakers raised the point of the implications of the enlargement of the Community for the likelihood of a European nuclear force. F. J. Strauss' vision of Europe is a European union, i.e. Western European, centered around a European nuclear force.

Prof. Brugmans: 'I do not know whether Strauss became a European because he wants a continental nuclear force or the other way round. But it is clear that he wants both a military and an economic union. Such a nuclear force would be a catastrophe. But being "against" something is not enough. The European federalists were against the French Force de Frappe and yet it is there. It is the weakness of the European Left to offer no alternative. This alternative does *not* lie in sabotaging or slowing down the proces of integration in order to prevent a nuclear force from coming into being, as is sometimes suggested. If there is a choice between a real option, though a deplorable one on the one hand and a political vacuum on the other, then history is not going to hesitate, whatever we do. But there *is* an alternative, which lies in the direction of functional World Federalism. There is, of course, the problem of Anglo-French nuclear co-operation when Britain joins the EEC, but the problem should be tackled then. It would not be a sensible policy to block British entrance for that reason.'

S. Patijn: 'The point is not so much Anglo-French co-operation, because their nuclear weapons, if not obsolete already will become so soon, since they do not have the means to update their weapon systems. But what will happen if Britain and France offer their force as a present to the Community? How do you keep the Germans and especially people like Strauss from accepting such a gift? That indeed would be a dangerous and disastrous development, which would immediately end all chances of a detente with the East and make the prospects for increased contact and co-operation very dim. They will not want to have anything to do with such a united Europe.'

DOES A UNITED WESTERN EUROPE POSE A THREAT TO THE EAST?

Ph. P. Everts: 'Johan Galtung argues, contrary to what John Pinder says in his paper, that a stronger EEC would prevent any co-operative and symmetrical deals with the East. Another thing is that developments in East and West are not only asymmetric but also asynchronic.

The West is ahead in economic development and institutionalisation. In the East the nation state is strong and in full bloom, in the West it is disintegrating and declining. Should the West not wait until the East has caught up, in order to make the relation more symmetric and co-operation more equally useful to both sides.'

J. Pinder: 'I may have sounded conservative, but I am not as conservative as to agree with Galtung about that.'

Prof. Brugmans: 'The Galtung thesis deserves closer scrutiny. What he is saying is that the larger a Community becomes, the more imperial and the less altruistic it becomes. Do you believe there is such a "law" either in political science or in economics?'

J. Pinder: 'I am sorry for having been so short but I was taken aback by the paradox that the Galtung thesis is so conservative. It would be true if the Community were very homogeneous, but it is not. In fact, it is so heterogeneous that the real danger is that of a reversal to the homogeneity of the nation-state, to oldfashioned nationalism. They are preventing the collective system from doing anything at all, rather than that the collective should acquire a frightening power. But of course it is large and could become a frightening power, and there would be a lot to be said for the imperialist thesis if the rest of the world consisted only of many small states, but it does not.

In the West there is the USA, in the East there is the Soviet Union. If the East consisted only of small states, I would be inclined to use our big guns only against the giants such as the US in the Kennedy Round and deal with the Eastern states on an individual bilateral basis.

But we should not forget that the Soviet Union is, after all, a big power, much more powerful than any of the Western European states, both in the strategic and the economic sense. Strategically it possesses for many years to come a more powerful military force than anything the West European countries could possibly mount, regardless of whether they tried to make a nuclear policy or not. In economic terms the SU is a substantial unit and it is growing. It seems to me hardly credible to argue that it is not in the interests of the Western countries to offer some counterweight.'

CHANGES IN EAST AND WEST

S. Patijn: 'In Pinder's paper it is suggested that it is difficult to see a bright perspective for Western investment in the East, because it does not fit into the economic system. But does it allow the many other

98

changes, which were mentioned as desirable and which some countries are now also experimenting with, like the Hungarians and the Yugoslavs? And is it fair to suggest that all the changes should take place on one side only?'

J. Pinder: 'It is not unrealistic to envisage a number of far reaching changes in many East European countries, some of which are discussed in the paper. The Yugoslavs and the Hungarians are doing just this, and it is very likely that they will continue. The last three years have been a period of transition, and the current reforms are now being digested. But the explicit intention is to go further. And there is no reason why they should go back on this, because they were a considerable success, and what they are doing is not against the basic principles of a Marxist-type economy. The tightly controlled economy of Stalinist Russia can be considered as an accident of history. It is not at all essential to the Marxist economy, as the example of Yugoslavia shows, which has got a large degree of decentralisation. Indeed it is not at all incompatible, as Oskar Lange showed, I think in 1936, to combine the use of markets with the public ownership of the means of production.

So it is likely that Hungary and Yugoslavia will continue and perhaps others will follow. The Czechs wanted to. Mr. Husak may be a Kadar and so perhaps may Mr. Gierek. It is not at all impossible and it would be very helpful to East-West economic relations.

Now what, on the other hand, are the changes that seem necessary and possible in the West? Here one is on much more speculative ground, because there has been nothing in the West to compare with the reforms in the East, like those in Hungary and Yugoslavia. The reason, of course, was that there was a much more pressing need for reform in purely economic terms. The system was cracking. The Czech economy was not growing. In the West, the phase of reform will, I think, come later. There are two things which seem necessary though, and which the Eastern economies can teach us.

One is the control of prices and the other is in the ownership of the means of production.

The Western economies will not be able to solve their price inflation. In our economies, where everything in the labour market is either oligopoly or monopoly, and where cost-push is therefore built in, we are just seeing the beginning of it. This problem is not going to be controlled without public control of prices and incomes.

The other thing is the ownership of the means of production. The existence of equity or share capital as a permanent institution compares with the latifundia which caused so much resentment against land-ownership in the past. The "absentee" equity owner can continue forever to get the surplus out of the company. The process of negotiation between East European authorities and Western firms may provide a useful answer, saying that these firms can have their profits and control, but only for fifty years, which after all is a long time. And some have suggested that this might indeed be an acceptable solution in the West also. It would enable the entrepreneur to build up something, but prevent the vast enterprises from passing on their surplus forever to people who perhaps do not really deserve this.'

W. Hager: 'It strikes me that very little has been said about the position of the Soviet Union. It seems probable that if developments are to follow their "normal" cause, we are going to deal much more with the Soviet Union, in the field of technology for instance and the East European countries may in fact find themselves between two economic and technological giants, unless we have a very deliberate policy of favoring these nations. But this seems a difficult policy to implement, economic interests being what they are, and with the Soviet Union being able to offer so much more to big Western firms than the small East European countries.'

J. Pinder: 'It is often ironic to see how much the natural forces exceed our efforts and power to implement our policies. One can think of the effect of preferential trade arrangements between the developing countries in the Commonwealth. The trade of these countries with the EEC increased much faster than their trade with Great Britain, and so it went with the Yaounde countries which increased their trade with Britain faster than their trade with the countries of the Community. The preferences were in one direction and the trade went in the other.

And this could also apply to Eastern Europe. But even if the effect were only partly successful, this is no reason not to try to prevent the development of the situation as described. But there are two questions here: would it not be better to be between two big powers than under one. The traditional position of the East-Europeans has been between Germany and Russia and this perhaps was better for them than to be under the hegemony of one or the other. The other question is in how far they will be able to follow the course which would be most profitable for them, which is to develop their own economic union, and common institutions, like the EEC has done. But the East Europeans are not near to it, and the Soviet Union obviously does not like the idea very much.'

100

J. Pinder: 'It may seem that there are differences between my words and those of Mozer with respect to the chances of influencing developments in the East. It would be dangerous to try to draw the East European countries away from the Soviet Union. But there are differences in the possibilities for an independent policy, which is clear if one looks at Hungary, Rumania and Yugoslavia. The policy of the Western countries should be to make it easy for Eastern Europe to make the necessary changes and reforms which are helpful to us. This is not a provocative stance, but a responsive one. As regards dealing with Comecon directly I do see problems. First of all, it does not have a common external policy. So there is not, at present, somebody to do business with. And if there were somebody to do business with, the sheer weight of the Soviet Union, which after all has two thirds of the population and half of the economy, would mean that you would really be doing business with the Soviet Union.

But all the same, many things can and should be done with the East Europeans. The important thing is not to exaggerate and not to provoke.'

G. L. Schim van der Loeff: 'Few people have asked the question, how much political and economic freedom for manoeuvre the countries of the West have relative to the US. And the same also applies to the Eastern countries with regard to the Soviet Union. Another question which should be discussed is: what are the political aims of the Soviet Union in the West? Does it aim to acquire an economic interest in the West through investments?'

A. Mozer: 'I see much freedom of action for the countries in the West, if only because there is no common trade and external policy vis-à-vis the East. Rivalry and bilateralism are the rule, whereby the Western countries are played off one against the other. In the East there is freedom of movement *within* an unassailable political conception. I do not know what the aims of the Soviet Union in the West are. It does have a number of agreements with countries like Italy, France and more recently Germany. Its main goal seems to be the maintenance of the status quo. In the West disintegration and bilateralism are prevailing. And on the other hand I see in its policies efforts to concentrate on particular countries to the point where Moscow has to consider this as an effort to break this particular country out of its bloc, leading to experiences of which the case of Czechoslovakia was

101

the latest example. To avoid such unacceptable policies, I am looking for common political concepts for the relations between West and East. In this respect much more is lacking in the West than in the East. The lack of solidarity and the fascination of short-term gains are the main reasons. But coexistence is in this way also endangered. Bilateralism should be dropped in favour of a common approach, which should first and foremost be a common approach to the Soviet Union. The lack of such a policy may provide dangers both for the West and for its relations with the East.'

THE POSITION OF THE EUROPEAN NEUTRALS

E. A. Alkema: 'I do not understand the position of Finland and would like to know why it does not, like some of the other neutrals, join the Council of Europe. It is after all a full member of OECD and membership in the Council of Europe is not really contradictory to its neutrality.'

S. Patijn: 'It seems clear how the neutral countries Finland, Austria and Yugoslavia could be related to the EEC. The most we can do is to offer preferential trade agreements, and ways should be found to work out such agreements with these countries. The situation is different however with respect to Sweden and Switzerland. They are not similar. Sweden has a foreign policy, while Switzerland wants to make it clear that it has not. I agree with Mozer that any kind of association for these countries is out of the question. It makes you a part of the Community without having anything to say on its policies. There is, for me, no reason why we should do anything for Sweden and Switzerland. It is not necessary to give preferential trade agreements, nor is it necessary to offer association. Full membership is rejected by both countries. Sweden has already said so, Switzerland will follow. So they will be left outside. I wonder if Mozer would agree that the only thing the EEC can offer is full membership and that if they reject that, it is their problem.'

A. Mozer: 'Finland is different from Austria in the sense that it has always rejected steps which it feared it could be made to retract under Soviet pressure. Membership of the Council of Europe is clearly such a political move, and I think it has not been considered important enough to risk political troubles. But membership would not be contradictory to its position of neutrality.

In the cases of Sweden and Switzerland I would be less extreme than

102

suggested before. It would be politically untactful if the EEC were to close its doors. It should be their responsibility to reject membership, if they do not want to comply with the requirements, and wish to retain their neutrality. It is their decision to take. But the practical result will probably be the same.'

P. J. Kapteyn: 'The problem is however that, if we accept the common external tariff, this implies discrimination against them. The US has always said it would accept the common tariff, if the EEC were to lead to a political union. They would not accept it in the case of a combination with EFTA. We, therefore, have obligations, because of the discriminatory nature of the tariffs and the likely loss of trade with the larger Community.'

P. A. Hausmann: 'There are some arguments on the Swiss side which should at least be mentioned. The Swiss would say, first of all, that their neutrality is much older than the EEC and secondly that Switzerland has a European and worldwide mandate – as Sweden in some respects also has – and that it plays its role for the benefit of Europe (and not only as a haven for foreign capital) as well as for the world at large. We should think, of course, of its role as the host of so many international organizations. This would also have to be taken into account.'

A. Mozer: 'These arguments support my point of view, that the Community should not say "no" in advance. If and when it comes to negotiations, all these arguments should be brought to bear. Then the Swiss (and the Swedes) should make up their minds and decide whether they prefer membership to the retention of their policy of neutrality or not.'

R. Cohen: 'I would support Mozer on this. Also we should not speak of preferences but of measures to counter the disadvantages resulting from the new situation for Sweden and Switzerland. In the agrarian field I find it difficult to conceive of concessions, because of the institutional arrangements and system of decisionmaking, but in the area of industrial products preferential arrangements are feasible and are being discussed.'

INSTITUTIONAL ARRANGEMENTS FOR EAST-WEST RELATIONS

J. Pinder: 'I am sceptical about the effect of Polish membership of the GATT. Is there a real increase in their trade due to their obligations under GATT?'

D. J. de Geer: 'It is interesting to note, that, whereas we have said that the Western countries should not deal separately with the Eastern countries, they are in fact doing this, witness Poland's entry into the GATT. Some say there is a strategy behind this. The Poles will ask for this concession, the Hungarians will ask for another and so on, and finally the Soviet Union will come and ask for all of them.'

J. Kaufmann: 'As always, it is difficult to say what might have been, but I think Polish membership of GATT is important. It is expected to lead to the abolition of the remaining quantitative restrictions by the Western countries, which are not permitted under the GATT. I find it impossible to speculate on a possible common strategy of East European countries on their relations with GATT, and I do not see any evidence of this.'

Part II

Europe and the developing countries

R. COHEN

The Treaty establishing the European Economic Community does not contain a single article on the Community's commitment vis-à-vis developing countries. Part Four of the Treaty, dealing with the association of overseas countries and territories, sets out the provisions ruling the relations between the Community and these countries and territories; but even from these provisions no general development policy can be derived. However, the Preamble to the Treaty states expressly that one of the considerations underlying the establishment of the Community was the intention to confirm the solidarity which binds Europe and the overseas countries and the desire to ensure the development of their prosperity, in accordance with the principles of the charter of the United Nations. 'Overseas countries' apparently refers to the associated countries because the Treaty does not mention any other overseas countries.

On the other hand, Article 110 of the Treaty states that 'by establishing a customs union between themselves Member States aim to contribute, in the common interest, to the harmonious development on international trade and the lowering of customs barriers'. If given a wide interpretation, this Article may be taken to suggest that the Community should, in principle, be able to develop a strategy for its trade relations with the developing countries. The same can be said of Article 238 of the Treaty, which deals with certain relations between the Community and third countries: 'The Community may conclude with a third state, a union of states or international organization agreements establishing an association involving reciprocal rights and obligations, common action and special procedures.' Article 238 only refers to 'third states' and does not specifically mention developing countries. The Article, therefore, has general validity and can be used to serve as a basis for relations with 'third states' in general, both industrialized and developing countries. In practice, however, the Article has been applied to establish relations between the Community and a number of developing countries. The same is true for Article 113, paragraph 3, which has also served as a basis for relations between the Six and a number of developing countries.

Part Four of the Treaty and Articles 110, 113 and 238 seem a narrow basis on which to found a development policy. But, from a historical point of view, it is not surprising that the Treaty contains very few indications for such a policy. When, fifteen years ago, the negotiations leading to the establishment of the European Economic Community were taking place (1955-57), 'development aid' was much less of a household word than nowadays. The term 'developing countries' had not yet been coined while a large number of countries which nowadays are called developing countries, especially in Africa and also Asia, were still colonies dependent on the mother countries and often involved in a struggle for independence and sovereignty. Political freedom, and not economic development, was the slogan of the day although, of course, these countries were in fact developing despite their dependent status. Under these circumstances, the inclusion of provisions on a common general development policy was not so obviously indicated as it is now – just as, in those days, no one in the Member States was thinking of making development affairs the responsibility of a special minister, or even of a junior minister.

In those early days, the Community's activity vis-à-vis developing countries was limited to obligations resulting from the association agreements with overseas countries and territories. Only gradually was the need felt for a more general development policy. Two parallel trends on the international scene gave rise to this need. When, in the sixties, almost all former colonies and dependent territories had acquired independence, the developing countries started to make economic demands themselves. These demands were formulated by individual countries but also, especially after the UNCTAD was founded, by the developing countries as a group. These countries' economic demands were addressed to individual industrialized countries but it soon became clear that, in the case of the Community's member countries, many of these demands should not be addressed to individual Member States but to the Community as a whole. For the Community's evolution towards a customs union and the gradual amplification of the common agricultural policy made it impossible for individual Member States to respond to many of the demands expressed by the developing countries. In view of these demands and of the Community's internal development, the Community began to consider the possibility and the desirability of a general development policy to complement existing relations with overseas countries and territories. In the meantime, especially since the opening of negotiations on the Community's enlargement, everyone has come to agree that a development policy *is* desirable and that it is now only a question of examining the possibilities. A Community consisting of at least ten highly industrialized West European countries with a common customs tariff, a common agricultural policy, and a common monetary policy in the making cannot ignore the question of its relations with the Third World.

The question of the possibilities of a development policy is also a question of available instruments and methods to be followed. Because of the limited instruments which the Community has, at this moment, at its disposal – various forms of association, food aid and tariff preferences – it is also a political question: are Member States prepared to provide the Community with the means necessary for pursuing a general development aid policy? No satisfactory reply can be given to this question because it largely depends on the course the Community will be taking in the near future and on the speed of Community developments. At present, we may attempt to examine the fields to be covered by a future development policy pursued by the enlarged Community. In order to do so, however, we must first give a brief outline of the Community's present relations with developing countries.

THE ASSOCIATION OF AFRICAN STATES AND MADAGASCAR

The official association of a number of African States and Madagascar with the European Community resulted from the fact that, when the Treaty of Rome was signed, these countries were still French colonies and, as such, enjoyed certain trade preferences on the French home market. The economic necessity to continue these preferences led to institution of the association system. The conditions of association were laid down in the Treaty establishing the European Economic Community which came into effect on 1 January 1958, viz. in Part Four of this Treaty and in the Implementing Convention annexed to it.

The system of association set out in the Treaty was characterized by the progressive establishment of a free trade area between the Community and the Associated States; by a number of provisions on freedom of establishment and freedom to supply services; and by Community financial aid to associated territories. The Implementing Convention was concluded for a five-year period.

In 1960-1962, these territories freed themselves from French domination and became independent states. With the single exception of Guinea, which also preferred not to become a member of the Communauté Française founded at the time, these territories declared that they wished to continue the association with the Community.

Negotiations between the Community and the countries eligible for association resulted in the Yaoundé Convention of July 1963. As a result of delay in the ratification procedures the Convention did not enter into force until 1 June 1964. There were a few important differences between the system laid down by the Yaoundé Convention and the Implementing Convention of the Rome Treaty. Not only had the political situation changed, but certain economic adjustments also turned out to be necessary. The altered political situation was reflected in the establishment of a number of association institutions: the Association Council, the Parliamentary Conference of Association and the Court of Arbitration. The economic adjustments had been made necessary by internal developments in the Community, especially the evolution of the common agricultural policy. The free trade principle of the association was maintained, characterized by the mutual granting of tariff preferences for industrial products and for some tropical products. In order to meet the wishes of other developing countries, however, the Community unilaterally reduced or abolished the preferences on a number of tropical products (coffee, tea, cocoa, tropical fur). Special trade arrangements, not specified further, were made for agricultural products from the Associated States which are comparable to or competitive with European farm products.

The abolition of a number of preferences and the establishment of new trade arrangements for certain agricultural products were partly compensated by an increase in financial aid. The Implementing Convention provided for 581.25 million units of account for financial aid; this amount was increased to 730 million units of account under the Yaoundé Convention. Part of this money was provided in the form of loans, totalling 110 million units of account, of which 46 million was granted by the European Development Fund itself on special favourable terms and 64 million by the European Investment Bank on normal terms.

In contrast to the provisions of the Implementing Convention, the financial resources available under the Yaoundé Convention could be used not only to finance economic and social investments but also for technical assistance in all its various forms, for measures of price support for various products, and for diversification of production. Like the Implementing Convention, the Yaoundé Convention (Yaoundé I) was concluded for a five-year period.

Simultaneously with the signing of the first Yaoundé Convention, a declaration of intent, adopted by the Council of Ministers of the European Communities as early as April 1963, came into effect. This declaration, which was meant to stress the 'open' character of the association, had been adopted mainly at the request of the Dutch and German Governments and made it possible for other African countries, besides the French-speaking ones, to conclude association agreements with the Community. The declaration states that non-member countries whose economic structure and production are comparable to those of the Associated African States and Madagascar can submit a request to:

i. accede to the Yaoundé Convention;
ii. conclude a separate association agreement;
iii. conclude a trade agreement.

Under this declaration of intent, negotiations on a form of association were soon opened with Nigeria and with three East African states: Kenya, Uganda and Tanzania.

As Yaoundé I had been concluded for a five-year period, expiring on 31 May 1969, the Convention included provisions that negotiations were to start in the course of 1968 to discuss a possible renewal of the association. These negotiations took place in 1968 and 1969 and led to the signing of a second Yaoundé Convention (Yaoundé II) on 29 July 1969. Ratification of the second Convention was likewise delayed a long time: Yaoundé II did not enter into force until 1 January 1971. The new Convention was also concluded for only five years, but with a fixed expiry date, 31 January 1975. By that date a new Convention must be concluded if the association is to continue. The present Convention stipulates that negotiations to that end should begin in the course of 1973.

The differences between Yaoundé II and Yaoundé I are smaller than those between Yaoundé I and the Implementing Convention. They all follow the trend already discernible in Yaoundé I: reduction of preferential arrangements; increase of financial aid to compensate this reduction; explicit recognition that the preferential arrangements should not be incompatible with the system of generalized preferences for developing countries which is to be set up under the UNCTAD programme.

Preference on coffee, cocoa and palm oil have again been reduced (from 9.6% to 7%, from 5.4% to 4%, and from 9% to 6%); financial aid has been increased from 730 million units of account to 918 million units of account. The associated countries' financial responsibility for their own development has increased because relatively more help is now given in the form of loans than in that of grants. Aid to production in the form of price support has been dropped and replaced

113

by *ad hoc* intervention in cases where world market price levels would threaten the normal implementation of the development programme. The possibility for the associated countries to waive the principle of 'reverse preferences' has been extended, especially where regional co-operation between associated countries might call for this. Such regional co-operation is encouraged in the Convention, for example in provisions meant to incorporate financial and technical assistance into regional co-operation programmes.

In general, financial assistance is viewed primarily as an instrument for increasing the agricultural and industrial capacity of associated countries. As is clear from the following small table, this trend has already been noticeable under Yaoundé I:

	First Development Fund	*Second Development Fund + Investment Bank*
Transport and communications	nearly 50%	under 30%
Agricultural production	under 20%	over 40%
Industrialization	about 1%	nearly 10%

Under the projects to be financed from the third Development Fund, this line will be pursued. The necessary means will consist of 810 million units of account made available from the Fund in the form of loans on special terms, and 90 million made available by the European Investment Bank as loans on normal terms. It has been stipulated explicitly that these two forms of loans, unlike the grants, can only be used for development schemes which are guaranteed to produce a profit.

Reverse preferences

The reverse preferences granted to the Community by the Associated African States and Madagascar cover various sectors: trade, freedom of establishment, freedom to supply services and free movement of payments and of capital. As regards the last four categories, the main provision is that rights granted by one Associated State to a particular Member State (i.e. France or Belgium) should also be granted to the other Member States.

The trade provisions stipulate that products originating in the Community should be imported exempt from customs duties, levies of

114

equivalent effect or quantitative restrictions. But there are many exceptions to these provisions. Each Associated State has the right to introduce or maintain customs duties or levies of equivalent effect in accordance with its economic or budgetary needs. A similar provision applies to quantitative restrictions on imports.

Moreover, the Associated States can maintain or bring about between themselves customs unions, free trade areas or economic cooperation agreements.

Customs unions, free trade areas or economic cooperation agreements can also be established with one or more third countries in Africa with a comparable level of development, or with third countries outside Africa. In the two latter cases, the Community can ask for discussion of the matter in the Association Council.

THE ASSOCIATION BETWEEN THE COMMUNITY AND THE THREE
EAST AFRICAN STATES OF TANZANIA, UGANDA AND KENYA

The African States of Tanzania, Uganda and Kenya together form the East African Community, established on 6 June 1967 when the East African Cooperation Treaty was signed at Kampala. Together these three countries form a customs union. As early as September 1963, a few months after the Council's declaration of intent, on the occasion of the signing of Yaoundé I, took effect, the three countries asked for negotiations on a separate association agreement with the Community.

After lengthy negotiations, an agreement was signed at Arusha on 28 July 1968 which never came into effect because on its date of expiry, 31 May 1969 (expiry date of Yaoundé I), it had only been ratified by the three East African countries themselves and by Belgium and the Netherlands.

The new aim was to conclude a new association agreement which would come into effect simultaneously with Yaoundé II. The first round of negotiations turned out to be useful because the new agreement could be worked out in a very short period (July 1969). This agreement, the Arusha Treaty, was signed on 24 September 1969 and entered into force on 1 January 1971, the same day as Yaoundé II. The agreement was concluded for a five-year period with a fixed expiry date (31 Januari 1975). Eighteen months before that date, negotiations can be started on a new agreement. These provisions, then, are analogous to those of Yaoundé II. Under the Treaty, an Association Council

115

has been established whose task it is to implement the objectives laid down in the agreement. The Court of Arbitration has also been retained, but the Parliamentary Conference of Association has been abolished. The only provisions in this respect are that contacts between the European Parliament and the national parliaments of the East African states are to be improved.

These institutional provisions, which are less far-reaching than those in Yaoundé II, are in line with the less far-reaching economic implications of the Arusha Treaty as compared to Yaoundé II. The provisions on freedom of establishment, freedom to supply services and free movement of payments and capital are comparable to those of Yaoundé II, but the Arusha Treaty does not contain any provisions on financial aid and the provisions on trade policy are likewise more restricted.

In principle, the free trade area concept has been retained in the Arusha Treaty: products originating from the three African countries can be imported freely into the Community and vice versa. Agricultural products from the African countries which are similar to and competitive with European products form an exception (as in Yaoundé II). A number of tropical products are also excepted. The concessions on imports into the Community do not include unroasted coffee, cloves or pineapple preserves. Each year, only 5.600 tons of coffee, 120 tons of cloves and 360 tons of pineapple preserves can be imported freely into the Community from the three East African states. Furthermore, it is stipulated that the Community, following consultation in the Association Council, can take steps if these annual quantities are exceeded and traditional trade flows are seriously threatened. Obviously these provisions have been included to protect the interests of the original Associated African States.

The remaining provisions of the Arusha Treaty correspond to those of the Yaoundé Agreement. The three East African countries can maintain or introduce customs duties, levies of equivalent effect or quantitative restrictions if they are necessary for their economic development or for budgetary purposes. They can, moreover, establish customs unions, free trade areas or economic agreements with third countries. It is further stipulated that the agreement does not stand in the way of the development of a general system of tariff preferences vis-à-vis developing countries.

In accordance with the limited content of the agreement, as compared with Yaoundé II, the reverse preferences granted to the Com-

116

munity are also less significant. The Community has been granted tariff preferences from 2% to 9% for about 60 products. This list of products can be amended, provided the total size of preferences and their equal distribution among the Member States of the Community are maintained.

NIGERIA

In September 1963, the Government of Nigeria submitted an official request to open negotiations for an association agreement with the Community, analogous to that of the East African countries. Negotiations were started in summer 1964 and the Treaty of Lagos was signed on 16 July 1966. This Treaty has never come into effect because it expired on the same day as Yaoundé I and it had not been ratified before that date (Biafra).

Since then, the Nigerian authorities have not submitted a new request for negotiations.

ASSOCIATION OF OVERSEAS COUNTRIES AND TERRITORIES

Annex IV of the Treaty contains a list of countries and territories to which the provisions of Part Four of the Treaty are to be applied.

The annex also contains the names of countries that have acquired independence over the years and which now fall under the Yaoundé Convention. Netherlands New Guinea is also mentioned in this annex, but since its transfer to Indonesia New Guinea no longer falls under the association system.

The other territories mentioned in the annex (e.g. Saint Pierre and Miquelon, the Comoro Archipelago, New Caledonia, French Settlements in Oceania, Southern and Antarctic territories) are still associated with the Community in the sense of Part Four of the Treaty. The Implementing Convention applied to these territories from 1 January 1958 to 31 December 1962. In February 1964, the Council of Ministers adopted a decision which, for the period covered by Yaoundé I, introduced arrangements for these territories which were more or less identical with those of Yaoundé I. The same procedure was followed for the period covered by Yaoundé II.

The differences between the association of the AASM and the association of the overseas countries and territories spring from the fact that the former are independent countries while the latter are not.

117

When the Treaty of Rome was signed, Surinam and the Netherlands Antilles could also have become associate members. The Netherlands Government, however, deemed a declaration of intent sufficient in which it was stipulated that the Community's countries were prepared to open negotiations in order to conclude economic association agreements with Surinam and the Netherlands Antilles. This procedure was preferred so as to avoid a delay in the signing of the Treaty which would have arisen from a provision in the Charter of the Kingdom of the Netherlands requiring that the Governments of Surinam and the Netherlands Antilles should be consulted before decisions on association agreements can be taken.

In the course of 1960, the Netherlands Government expressed the wish to make use of the possibility formulated in the Declaration of Intent.

The association of Surinam, whose economic structure resembles that of the African countries, did not present any special problems. The Council of Ministers simply decided by unanimous vote that Surinam was to have the same status as the overseas countries and territories. The association came into effect on 1 September 1962, and since that date Surinam has been included in the list of Associated Overseas Countries and Territories.

The association of the Netherlands Antilles was somewhat more difficult, because the Antilles was not considered as similar to African countries in its economic structure, and because the oil industry presented a special problem. A special Convention had to be concluded to enable the Antilles to enjoy the advantages of Part Four of the Treaty. Since 1 October 1964, the Netherlands Antilles has been an associate member and has been included in the list of Associated Overseas Countries and Territories.

Exceptions to the free trade principle were laid down in a separate petroleum protocol. Imports of petroleum products from the Netherlands Antilles into the Community are restricted to a fixed annual quantity.

French Overseas Departments (Réunion, Guadeloupe, Martinique, French Guiana)

Special arrangements for these Overseas Departments are formulated in Article 227 of the Treaty and Article 16 of the Implementing Convention. The validity of these arrangements was extended by Yaoundé I and II.

AGREEMENTS CONCLUDED BY THE COMMUNITY WITH COUNTRIES
IN THE MEDITERRANEAN AREA

The agreements concluded by the Community with countries in the Mediterranean basin can be divided into:
i. preferential agreements
ii. non-preferential agreements

The preferential agreements form the largest group and are, of course, the most important ones, both from an economic and a political point of view. They can be further subdivided into two categories: they are either association agreements under Article 238 of the Treaty or preferential trade agreements under Article 113 of the Treaty.

Agreements under Article 238

Country	Duration	Entry into force	Date of expiry
Greece	Unlimited	1.11.1962	—
Turkey	Unlimited	1.12.1964	—
Tunisia	Five years	1. 9.1969	31.8.1974
Morocco	Five years	1. 9.1969	31.8.1974
Malta	Five years	1. 4.1971	31.3.1976

Agreements under Article 113

Country	Duration	Entry into force	Date of expiry
Spain	Six years	1.10.1970	30.9.1976
Israel	Five years	1.10.1970	30.9.1975
UAR			
Lebanon			

With the exception of the agreements with Greece and Turkey, which expressly, though after a certain period, require the establishment of a customs union, the agreements under Article 238 are more like preferential trade agreements under Article 113 as far as their economic content is concerned. It is therefore impossible to conclude, on the basis of the Article underlying the agreement, that one agreement is of greater economic importance than the other. The preference of one article to the other is the expression of the Community's political pre-

119

ference at the time when the agreement was made rather than an attitude determined by economic considerations.

The preferences granted under the association agreements with Tunisia and Morocco, based on Article 238, are in practice only slightly more than the preferences granted to Spain and Israel. Tunisia and Morocco are, admittedly, exempt from duties on most industrial products; but these exports involve very small quantities. It is very well possible that the preferences of 70%, 40%, 50% and 28-34% respectively for a number of industrial products, granted to Spain and Israel for the period of the agreement, will turn out to be more important. There are considerable differences between the concessions made on agricultural products (especially citrus fruits, olive oil and wine) to Tunisia and Morocco, on the one hand, and to Spain, Israel and Turkey on the other. In practice, however, the economic significance of these preferences will be more or less the same, given the different starting position of the countries concerned. Before the Community was established, Tunisia and Morocco enjoyed full preferential arrangements on the French market and therefore have a preference – albeit smaller – throughout the Community's wider customs area. Spain, Israel and Turkey did not enjoy any preference on the French market and therefore enjoy a more restricted preference in the Community than Tunisia and Morocco. The Commission of the European Communities has always justified the existence of differences in preferences with the argument that it is desirable to maintain a certain balance among Mediterranean countries which are in competition with each other in the manufacture of identical products.

In principle, Greece has been granted the most far-reaching preferential arrangements, coupled with a form of financial aid. Political developments in Greece since April 1967, however, have caused the Community to take a more reserved attitude towards the Treaty concluded with this country. Financial aid to Greece has been discontinued, and the Commission is limiting itself to dealing with current matters expressly provided for in the agreement, without striving to extend the arrangements. This means that, in particular, the self-executing provisions of the agreement – e.g. on the intra-Community system for industrial products – are being carried out but that no further measures are being taken to implement the liberalization of trade in cases where additional decisions are required.

In the case of Turkey, the object of the agreement is likewise the establishment of a complete customs union. However, the transition period laid down for the achievement of this aim is so long (12 to 22 years) that the practical preferential treatment of Turkey does not amount to much at the moment. On the other hand, Turkey does receive financial aid.

In principle, Malta, as a European state, is also eligible for full membership. The association agreement, however, does not anticipate this possibility, with all its institutional consequences. A customs union is to be established with Malta in a two-stage transition period of 10 years. During the first stage of five years, the Community will reduce its import tariffs on industrial products by 70%.

At the moment, negotiations are in progress with the United Arab Republic and Lebanon on a preferential agreement under Article 113 of the Treaty. It is expected that these agreements will be signed within a few months.

Early in March 1971, preliminary talks began with Cyprus. As far back as 1962, in the context of the enlargement negotiations which were going on at he time, Cyprus had made a request for negotiations on its future relations with the Community; in 1970 Cyprus repeated this request. The Cyprus Government aims at an association with the Community, the exact nature of which has not yet been defined; a satisfactory solution of the problem of citrus and wine exports to the Community is the main objective.

Preliminary talks have also started with Portugal for the purpose of ascertaining the form which future relations could take. As an EFTA member, Portugal fears to lose its EFTA preferences after the Community's enlargement. And there are other reasons why Portugal wishes for closer ties with the Community (all countries in competition with Portugese production have, in one way or another, established links with the Community).

The situation is somewhat more complicated in the case of Algeria. As it formed part of French territory when the Rome Treaty was signed, most provisions of the Treaty also applied to Algeria (see Article 237 of the EEC Treaty). Since it became independent, no legally satisfactory basis has been established for the Community's relations with this country. The Algerian Government has asked the Community to open negotiations in order to conclude an association agreement which would regulate trade relations and economic and financial co-operation

121

and would also include provisions on the treatment of Algerian workers in the Community's territory. The Commission has urged the Council to start negotiations with Algeria as soon as possible, especially in order to establish trade relations; so far, the Commission has not yet been granted a mandate to negotiate.

The non-preferential agreements with Mediterranean countries have been concluded under Article 113.

Country	Duration	Entry into force	Date of expiry
Lebanon	Three years	1.7.1968	30.6.1971
Yugoslavia	Three years	1.5.1970	30.4.1973

The agreement with Lebanon includes non-preferential trade provisions under which Lebanon enjoys most-favoured-nation treatment (Lebanon is not a member of GATT), and a number of provisions on the coordination of technical co-operation. The Lebanese Government, however, is not very satisfied with this agreement. At the moment, negotiations for a preferential agreement are in progress. The agreement with Yugoslavia is a non-preferential trade agreement under which tariff reductions as agreed upon in the Kennedy Round will be speeded up for certain major Yugoslav exports. In addition, a special duty will be levied on a special kind of beef (baby beef) important for Yugoslavia's exports; furthermore, export price guarantees for wines have been fixed in order to prevent these products from being subject to a compensating levy.

Reverse preferences

All agreements concluded with Mediterranean countries contain provisions giving the Community a privileged access to these countries' markets. These reverse preferences are, of course, most extensive in the case of countries with which a customs union is to be established.

For industrial products, the Community usually dismantles its tariffs faster than the associated countries. For agricultural products, preferences have been determined for each product separately. In the case of preferential agreements not aiming at a complete customs union, reverse preferences have been established for each product or category of products separately. The agreement between the Community and Israel, for instance, contains five different lists of products, showing those which can be imported into Israel free of duty and those which

122

are subject to levies of 90%, 85%, 75% or 70% of the Israeli customs tariff.

Under the association agreement with Malta, Malta will reduce its customs tariff by 15% for a number of Community export products on the date of entry into force of the agreement, to be followed by a 25% reduction at the beginning of the third year and 35% at the beginning of the fifth year.

Similar provisions are included in the other agreements. Generally speaking, the importance of the reverse preferences demanded by the Community depends on that of the concessions granted by the Community.

GENERAL CHARACTERISTICS OF ASSOCIATION POLICY

The most important feature of this form of developing policy in the association agreements with the African States and Madagascar is the combination of financial aid and preferential trade arrangements. Trade and aid have been combined under one single policy and this financial aid is multilateral.

The fact that aid is multilateral is very important: it ensures that aid will be continued even if relations between an associated country and its former mother country or another Member State are temporarily endangered by political unrest. Financial aid is mainly granted for development projects; a request for the financing of a specific development scheme must be initiated by the associated country concerned. Aid for projects, however, is being increasingly combined with technical assistance, in accordance with the recommendations of the Pearson Report. Technical assistance may either be linked up with execution of the project itself, as a pre-investment, or take the form of a scheme for financing staff training.

The second important characteristic of the association system is its institutional structure. In particular, the parliamentary assembly of the association, although it has no powers, is unique in its kind. Naturally, this parliamentary contact was inspired by French views – even in the colonial era representatives of the overseas territories sat in the National Assembly – but its significance reaches far beyond the wish to maintain historic continuity. This contact is especially valuable in that it offers the possibility of exerting pressure on the national governments represented in the assembly. This pressure works two ways: European members of the assembly are directly confronted with the needs of their African counterparts while African representatives come to realize that, apart from the association interests, other aspects of development also demand attention.

In conclusion, association may be considered a unique form of development co-operation in that it combines trade and aid under the supervision of special institutions.

It is difficult to evaluate exactly the economic significance of the association relationship. (This does not apply to financial aid but to preferential trade relations.) It is clear that exports from the Associated African States and Madagascar to the Community have increased considerably. In 1958, the value of these countries' exports to the Community totalled $ 896 million; by 1969, this had increased to $ 1,718 million, corresponding to an average increase of 6% per year. This percentage, however, is below the percentage of the increase of exports to third countries (6.8%) and also below the increase of exports from other developing countries to the Community (7.1%). But if petroleum and petroleum products are excluded from these overall figures it is found that, especially in 1968 and 1969, exports from the associated countries have increased more than exports from other developing countries (5.1%). It is remarkable that the increase of exports from the Associated States to Member States which formerly had no relations with them is much greater than the increase of the Associated States' exports to France. In 1959, over 53% of total exports from the Associated States still went to France; at the moment, this has fallen to almost 40%. Exports from France and Belgium to these countries have also fallen; but exports from Germany have increased, and those from Holland and Italy have even more than doubled. In other words, the association system has helped to make trade between the Community and the countries concerned more intensive and multilateral while, at the same time, exports from other developing countries to the Community have not decreased. An overall evaluation of the results of the association between the Community and the African States and Madagascar can be made because this relationship has been in existence for over a decade; on the other hand, it is much harder to make such an evaluation for the association with the countries of the Arusha Treaty and of the Mediterranean basin. Under these associations, no financial aid is granted, and the association under the Arusha Treaty has only been in forse since 1 January 1971.

124

The same can be said of associations and preferential trade agreements in the Mediterranean area. Greece, at any rate, is a special case. As for Turkey, the second stage of the treaty with this country started only a few months ago. The preferential treaties with Spain and Israel came into force as recently as 1 October 1970. Only the association with Morocco and Tunisia has been in existence for a relatively longer period, but still not long enough for a proper judgement to be made. All that can be said is that trade relations between these countries and the Community show a favourable development without appearing to harm the interests of other countries.

OTHER COMMUNITY ACTIVITIES CONCERNING DEVELOPING COUNTRIES

A. *Generalized preferences*

Like other industrialized countries, the European Community has declared its readiness to introduce generalized tariff preferences on a unilateral basis for the benefit of developing countries, as agreed upon under the UNCTAD programme. The Community's arrangements are as follows:

1. *General system for industrial products and semi-finished products:*
Exemption from import duties up to a certain maximum quantity per year. On the basis of the 1968 import figures, developing countries can increase imports exempt from duties by 5% per year of the imports of the same products from industrialized countries. Beyond this quantity, normal tariffs are charged.

2. *General system for processed agricultural products:*
   i. For products which fall under a levy system with a fixed element, a reduction of 50% or 25% of the fixed element, depending on the product, is granted;
   ii. A tariff reduction of 20% or 10% is granted on products for which there is a customs tariff, depending on the product.

The tariff preferences will be valid from 1 July 1971. The countries eligible for preferences are sometimes referred to as the 'Group of 77' although, in reality, they number about 90 countries.

B. *Food aid*

Wheat
The Community is party to the International Wheat Agreement of 1967, by which it has undertaken to provide food aid. During the period in which the Agreement is valid (i.e. till 30 June 1971), the Community will provide 1.035.000 tons of wheat per year as food aid.

Negotiations on a new International Wheat Agreement have just been completed. The Agreement has been extended for a three-year period in which the food aid programme will be continued. Under certain circumstances, food aid in the form of wheat can be replaced by food aid in the form of rice. Requests for food aid received by the Community greatly exceed its contractual obligations.

Milk powder – butteroil
In 1970 the Community decided of its own accord to provide food aid in the form of milk powder and butteroil as well. These products are mainly supplied through international organizations such as the World Food Programme, under the auspices of FAO, or the International Red Cross Committee (about 120.000 tons of milk powder and about 35.000 tons of butteroil).

C. *Geographically restricted activities*

Asia
In May 1970, an agreement was concluded with Pakistan on the application of a duty-free tariff quota for silk and cotton. There is a quota of $ 1 million per year for both products. In addition, a tariff quota of $ 5 million has been introduced for handicrafts. Negotiations on the application of this quota have already been completed with Pakistan. Negotiations with Ceylon, Indonesia, Iran, India, the Philippines and Thailand are planned for the future.

India has requested the opening of negotiations in order to conclude an agreement on 'cooperation in the field of trade'. This request must be seen in the light of the negotiations on enlargement of the Communities. In 1964, following the negotiations with the United Kingdom, an agreement was reached with India exempting tea and pepper from duties.

Latin America
As early as February 1969, Argentina asked for negotiations to be

opened for the conclusion of a trade agreement. In November 1970, the Commission was given a mandate to open negotiations which, at this moment, are still in progress.

Uruguay, too, has asked for negotiations but even preliminary talks have not yet started.

The Andean group of countries (Bolivia, Chile, Colombia, Ecuador and Peru) have asked for a Joint Committee to be set up, consisting of representatives of the European Communities and of the Andean countries, to examine the problem that may arise in relations between the Community and these countries. They have also asked for technical assistance, especially in the sphere of economic integration. The application is under examination at the moment.

The South American countries are generally interested in strengthening their ties with the Community. In the Declaration of Buenos Aires (July 1970), the South American countries expressed the wish to conclude general trade agreements and to receive financial assistance from the Community. They have asked for help from the European Investment Bank, e.g. in the form of interest subsidies; co-ordination of the Member States' bilateral programmes; and technical assistance from the Community in its own special fields (e.g. economic integration, provision of scholarships and training courses).

The Community has not yet taken any decision on these applications and requests. In November 1970, however, the Council decided to apply the full tariff reduction on fifteen farm products, of special importance to the South American countries, as from 1 January 1971, i.e. one year earlier than had been agreed in the Kennedy Round.

GENERAL POSITION OF THE COMMUNITY AS AN INTERNATIONAL
TRADE PARTNER

The Community is already the world's most important market for exports from developing countries. In general, trade relations between the Community and these countries are developing favourably. The Community's balance of trade with the developing countries has always been negative, and the deficit is steadily increasing.

(in $ million)

	Imports cif	Exports fob
1958	6 824	6 125
1964	9 843	6 892
1970	16 004	11 133
	(estimate)	(estimate)

The increase of Community imports from the developing countries (83%) between 1958 and 1968 was smaller than that of total imports (108%). As a result, the developing countries' share in extra-Community imports fell from 42% to 37% between 1958 and 1968. At the same time, the structure of imports from developing countries changed considerably. Imports of food and raw materials increased by 22% and 33% respectively. On the other hand, imports of petroleum and petroleum products increased by 158%; the share of these products in total imports went up from 29% to 41%. Consequently, Libya is now the Community's most important supplier among the developing countries ($ 1.300 million in 1968), followed by Algeria ($ 770 million), Kuwait (720), Saudi Arabia (660) and Iraq (640). Brazil ranks sixth with $ 580 million (1968) followed at a great distance by countries like India or the Associated African States and Madagascar together.

In the same period, imports of industrial products from the developing countries doubled, going up from 8% to 16% of total imports. Nevertheless, it must be admitted that the total quantity of these industrial imports has remained small. They are small in two respects: (a) they make up just over 4% of the Community's total imports of these products; (b) in comparison with other industrialized countries, the Community imports relatively small quantities of them from the developing countries (compared with the United States, the United Kingdom, Norway, Sweden, Japan, etc.). Furthermore, imports of industrial products from the developing countries are also increasing in Germany and the Netherlands, which was hardly the case before, and it is to be expected that the Community will make a good showing in this respect within a few years. The Community's offer of generalized preferences (UNCTAD), and its willingness to apply these as early as 1 July 1971, point in that direction. The Community's offer of preferences for all industrial products (without exception) amounts to a basic import value of about $ 500 million (basis 1968); the permitted annual increase of 5% will also amount to an import value of $ 500 million. The Community's offer is less generous for imports of processed farm products under the general UNCTAD preference programme. Very many agricultural products are excepted, and the total import value of products coming under the preference system is only slightly above $ 30 million. The main reason for this relatively small offer is the fact that the Community has to defend its own agricultural interests; another reason is that the Community has already committed itself in other ways. Indeed, there is no other industrial country which has so many agricultural interests to defend as the Community. Products from

128

the temperate zone are produced in the Community itself; Mediterranean products are produced in countries which have, almost without exception, already concluded preferential agreements with the Community while tropical products are imported from the Yaoundé and Arusha countries.

It should be borne in mind, moreover, that the Community already imports considerable quantities of agricultural products. In 1969, the Community's total agricultural imports amounted to more than $ 8.000 million, of which almost half were imported from developing countries (not including the 'European' developing countries like Greece, Spain, Turkey, Portugal and Yugoslavia); of these $ 4.000 million, about $ 1.200 million were imported from countries enjoying a preferential agreement with the Community (Yaoundé, Arusha, Maghreb). These figures show that the Community is the world's most important importer of agricultural products. The Community alone received more than a quarter of all agricultural exports of all developing countries; about one third of all agricultural imports from developing countries is exempt from customs duties, levies or any other import charges.

The Community's trade with developing countries, therefore, does not show such a bad picture as is sometimes suggested; but it is obvious that there is still much room for improvements. These improvements will have to be considered, especially after the Community's enlargement by the addition of the United Kingdom, Ireland, Norway and Denmark.

The European Community is the world's most important trading power (including intra-Community trade), taking up about 20% of the world's total imports and exports; it is followed by the United States (18.5%), the United Kingdom (8.5%) and Japan (8%).

It is interesting to take a look at these figures in historical perspective. In 1956, two years before the establishment of the European Economic Community, the United States was the world's leading trade partner (15%) followed by the United Kingdom (about 10%). At the time, the countries that were soon to form the European Economic Community already accounted for just over 20% of total world trade; but this percentage included trade between them. In 1956, Japan's share in world trade was only about 3%.

These figures show that the four leading trading powers of today had much smaller shares in world trade 15 years ago. The figures also show that an enlarged Community would have a dominant influence on international trade: it would represent over a quarter of total world trade.

The accession of the four candidate countries would also have an important impact on the relations between the European Community and the developing countries. In 1966, total exports from all developing countries to the Community ('the Six') amounted to $ 11.642 million. In 1967, this had gone up to $ 11.931 million. Expressed in percentages, this means that the exports of all developing countries together to the Community of the Six represented 30.4% (1966) and 30.1% (1967) of their total exports. If the Community of Six had, at that time, already been a 'Community of Ten', the percentages would have been 43.6 and 43.2 respectively. The figures of imports from the Community to developing countries show a similar picture. In 1966, these amounted to $ 8.469 million and in 1967 to $ 9.029 million, or 21.2% and 21.6% of total imports.

For a Community of Ten, these figures would have been 31.2% and 30.7%. Of course, these figures must be viewed with caution and cannot be taken as basis for extrapolation over subsequent years.

The present Community is of considerable importance to developing countries, and an enlarged Community will be even more important. This prospect gives rise to a number of problems. The enlarged Community cannot just continue the policy vis-à-vis developing countries which is pursued by the present Community.

Some of the necessary changes in this policy will be made during the negotiations on enlargement. As an example, we may quote the solution that has to be found for sugar exports from developing countries which are party to the Commonwealth Sugar Agreement. A partial solution, at any rate in principle, may also be found to problems concerning those developing countries of the Commonwealth that are eligible for association. The question to what extent these countries' economic problems will, in fact, be solved by association agreement will depend on the particular form of association (Yaoundé, Arusha or *ad hoc*).

If all countries eligible for association were to conclude an association agreement with the enlarged Community, the Community will have preferential trade relations with about 50 countries. If all these countries are to be given equal treatment, the countries which are, at the moment, most favoured by the preferential system, those of the Yaoundé Treaty, will lose some of their privileges. To avoid this, differentiated preferences could be resorted to; such a differentiated system exists at present for the Yaoundé and Arusha countries. Alter-

130

natively, an entirely new preferential system may be set up, e.g. by combining several association systems already existing for the associated countries of the Community and for the Commonwealth countries. It would, finally, also be possible to revise the association or preferential relations with the Mediterranean countries.

Another reason for revising the Community's association policy would be the dissatisfaction which this policy is causing among other industrialized countries, especially the United States. The objections raised to it by the United States should, however, be studied properly. If the Community had already been enlarged in 1969 and agreement had been reached on the association of all eligible African and Caribbean countries, the imports from all associated countries into the enlarged Community would not have exceeded 7% of total imports, and exports to those countries would not have been more than about 5% of total exports.

It is hard to predict at this point whether the countries involved will be willing to change the association system. It may be expected that, in the following years, attempts will be made to amend existing agreements. In the short term, a revision of the Community's generalized UNCTAD preferences is more important. This revision is necessary if only because the offers of the United Kingdom, Ireland, Norway and Denmark have to be incorporated into the Community's overall offer. At the same time, the qualitative and quantitative aspects of the Community's offer should be revised in view of the important role the enlarged Community will play as a market for the developing countries. In the longer term, this means that the Community will have to pursue internal industrial and agricultural policies which will make such preferences possible. The implementation of the Mansholt-plan for agriculture, for instance, is essential in this respect.

CONCLUSION

It is clear that the relationships between the European Communities and a number of developing countries have mainly been determined by a number of historical and political factors. This is true for the African countries south of the Sahara and those in the Mediterranean area. The relationship with African countries south of the Sahara is a direct consequence of ties that existed between them and certain Member States prior to the establishment of the Community, and of Part Four and the Implementing Convention of the Treaty which were the outcome of these ties.

The relationship with a number of Mediterranean countries is, at least in part, also based on the 'Declaration of Intent with a view to the association of the independent countries of the franc area with the European Economic Community', which forms part of the Treaty. This Declaration has served as a basis for negotiations with Morocco and Tunisia which ultimately led to their association with the Community.

The association agreements with Greece and Turkey cannot be explained from historical circumstances; they were concluded for political reasons. After the establishment of the European Communities and the European Free Trade Association, with Finland and Portugal as 'associate members', Greece and Tureky were left as the only European countries that did not belong to an economic bloc.

The extension of the association system in Africa and round the Mediterranean was mainly a result of the fact that associations as such already existed. After the deadlock reached in the first round of negotiations for enlargement (1961-63), the Council's declaration of intent seemed an adequate basis on which to open up the association system and also admit countries other than French-speaking African ones.

The extension of the association system in the Mediterranean area is also, in a sense, more or less a coincidence and can only be explained from the fact that certain association agreements had already been concluded. Greece, Turkey, Morocco and Tunisia were already associate members. Their main competitors were, and are, countries like Israel, Spain, Lebanon, the United Arab Republic, Algeria, Cyprus and Malta; so, as soon as these latter countries expressed the wish to establish closer links with the Community, the most obvious solution was to extend the association system to cover them. In fact, this association system is not based on a deliberate policy. The concept of 'association' is not defined in the Treaty, or hardly, and various political preferences of Member State Governments in fact determined the policies vis-à-vis developing countries. Some people, for instance, considered that Spain needed help through association or a preferential agreement. Others replied that, in that case, the same had to be done for Israel. In this way, almost all the countries along the northern and southern Mediterranean coasts gradually came to have special relations with the Community. Because the term 'association' had not been defined in the Treaty and because the Treaty did not contain any provisions on development policy – apart from Part Four and the Implementing Convention – the contents of association treaties and preferential agreements were determined by the Community's present status: a customs union for industrial and agricultural products with a common financial responsibility for farm policy. Of course, the Community is developing towards closer unity, but this trend has not yet gone so far that specific responsibilities for Community relations with third countries can be derived from it.

In the short term, enlargement of the Community by the accession of the United Kingdom, Ireland, Denmark and Norway will not change this situation. The negotiations take a long time, and it will also take some time before the new Member States have adjusted themselves to the Community system. It can therefore not be expected that time, energy and ideas will be available to reorganize relations between the Community and the developing countries before the negotiations are completed or even soon afterwards. Nevertheless, due thought must be given to the way in which the enlarged Community of the future will entertain relations with the developing countries. The accession of the United Kingdom means a reinforcement of the existing situation: the United Kingdom, too, has special ties with many developing countries under the Commonwealth system. It is obvious that these countries will want association with the enlarged Community. In fact, agreement has already been reached during the negotiations on an extension of the association system to eight African countries. It is very well possible that the enlarged Community will ultimately have association or preferential agreements with some 50 developing countries in Africa, the Mediterranean basin and the Caribbean. Unfortunately, the more countries are granted preference, the less effective these preferences are. One of the consequences of this fact has been that, in the case of East Africa, a quota system for a number of products was introduced to protect the interests of the Yaoundé countries. Similar difficulties will no doubt be encountered if the association system is extended to even more countries. This consideration is, or at least should be, sufficient reason for reviewing association policy before proceeding further.

In view of these considerations, the enlarged Community will have to re-examine its attitude towards and relations with developing countries. The extension of the association system among the African and Mediterranean countries should have been an opportunity for such a re-examination but, as it happened, very few changes were made. The entry of the United Kingdom gives the Community a unique opportunity for reconsidering its responsibilities towards the Third World.

The European Community and the developing countries seen in global perspective

H. A. J. COPPENS

'There is a widespread assumption that "political neutrality" is the first prerequisite of objective science. This view defines objectivity in science, not in terms of whether its theories are tested but in terms of a political stand that is supposed to be neutral. In the first place, there is no such thing as political neutrality; all science has implications for or against the present social order. Secondly, the unwitting introduction of political criteria into scientific method makes the resulting "science" a form of politics in disguise'.

(Robin Jenkins, Exploitation, the world power structure and the inequality of nations, 1970, p. 29.)

INTRODUCTION

The organisers of this symposium have asked me to examine the relationship between the European Community and the developing countries from the global point of view, obviously assuming that this would yield different conclusions from those reached when approaching the problem from a European perspective. I hope they will be proved wrong in this, for I believe that in our 'small' world of today, Dutch and European interests coincide with world interests. For the same reason I consider that what are called the development problems are not problems that exist only in the developing countries. By definition the problem of development is a global problem, since the rich can be called rich only because there are the poor. But also, because the rich countries are hampering the development of the poor countries in countless ways, even making it impossible here and there. I shall be dealing with this in greater detail later on.

In chapter I a diagram is given of the global perspective, which in subsequent chapters serves as an interpretation framework for the functioning of the (enlarged) European Community in the world, particularly as regards the position of the developing countries in it. In chapter II the Community of the Six is examined as to its relations with the developing countries; special attention being given to the import, agricultural and association policy. Another matter discussed there is the General System of Preferences, which will become operative in the near future. Chapter III considers some of the effects the enlargement of the European Community will have on the economies of the developing countries. Lastly, in chapter IV a few general conclusions are drawn, that lead us to a 'harsh' verdict on the Community.

137

With a little imagination it is possible to picture what would happen if the physical centre of gravity of our globe were to shift so as to correspond with the politico-economic balance of power of the countries. The earth's centre of gravity would come to lie in the Northern Hemisphere, the more or less regular rotation of the earth would change into the lurching gait of a drunk, and our world would sail through space like a planet that has lost its bearings. Experts would be able to predict what natural catastrophies this would lead to, and whether the inhabitants of the earth had any chances of survival.

Such crazy thoughts are only entertained in science fiction. And yet we may well ask ourselves whether it really is so strange that such thoughts occur to us, when we take a look at the global community of today. There can be no doubt that the politico-economic centre of gravity of Mother Earth is located in the Northern Hemisphere. Some aspects of this will be reviewed in the following passages. This lack of equilibrium may not result in natural disasters (although we cannot even be sure of this, considering the increasing pollution of the environment and the serious disturbance of the natural balance in the industrial areas), but one question that does arise is what are mankind's chances of survival if the present inequalities continue unchanged or are even amplified?

a. *The hierarchic international system*

The international system, in the sense of a functional arrangement of related and interconnected parts of an entity, is hierarchic in its structure. The elements of the system are formed by the national states, which represent a specific form of human organisation (but one might just as well examine other specific forms of human organisation as to their role in the international system; for instance, the multinational enterprise). The functional arrangement is evident in the world-encompassing capitalist system, which displays a large measure of cohesion and interdependence. The same holds good for the communist system, which covers a smaller part of the earth's surface.

In the international juridical sense and also in common parlance, a national state is a sovereign unit which maintains relations with other sovereign units on the basis of equality and equivalence. In this context Johan Galtung speaks of a 'billiard ball image of nations'. This image does not correspond with the reality of the present-day international community. States differ from one another in many respects; they are

138

distinguishable not only in geographic size and location, but also in their economic and/or political pattern and structure. These differences play a major role in their mutual relations. Their inequality also rules out any question of equivalence.

It is true that in certain circumstances states formally have equal say (as in the UN Assembly), and that countries of unequal power may conclude agreements on a basis of equality. It would, however, be misleading to suppose that such formal equality between the national states covered their true relations (even though formal equality can sometimes counterbalance – albeit inadequately – existing de facto inequalities).

The international system, on the contrary, is characterised by a markedly hierarchic structure[1], in which the national states have different ranks in accordance with their political, economic, technological and cultural power. Power in this context means a state's capacity to exercise influence over other states[2]. In his article in *Internationale Spectator* Sideri describes the international system as a pyramidal structure:

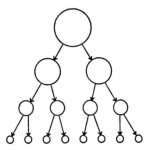

The direction of the arrows in this figure indicates that the lower regions are influenced more by decisions and changes at the top, than conversely. This means that the relations in the international system are *asymmetric*. Besides the aforementioned *inequality* of the parts (by reason of which their place in the order of the system may be deduced) an important characteristic is the predominant *verticality* in the relations between them (in the sense that, notably in the lower regions, the horizontal relations are weak).

b. *Historical development of the system*

In former times the reality of the relations between states fitted better into the pattern outlined above than in present times. Oliver C. Cox

139

describes how the rise and fall of the various trading centres (including Holland), were followed by a world-wide integration under British leadership. 'The system apparently reached its highest state of perfection between 1870 and the First World War'[3]. Cox arranges the countries in their order of importance at that time, using as classification criterion: the extent to which a country is able to control its external trade relations. He distinguishes between the following five ranks: (1) Leaders, (2) Subsidiaries, (3) Progressives, (4) Dependents, and (5) Passives. At that time Great Britain, the United States and Germany represented the absolute top, followed in the second rank by the other major European powers and Japan. In the lowest regions are the 'dependents', countries which, though possessing political independence, have a large measure of dependence through being within the sphere of influence of the great powers. The 'passives' are the colonised nations of that time. Their economies were arranged to meet the wishes and requirements of the 'mother countries'; they were the suppliers of raw materials and tropical foods, and functioned as markets of the industrialised nations.

After World War I the first changes became evident in this highly integrated global system. The Russian revolution took a big bite of territory out of the system. After World War II, when the European powers fell back into the second level, the United States became the undisputed leader of the capitalist world. The Soviet Union greatly expanded its sphere of influence and constituted a new hierarchic system. For some time China also formed part of it, but this state of affairs was ended by the cooling off and subsequent rupture between Moscow and Peking.

The decolonisation after World War II brought the suppressed nations of the Third World independence in the formal sense only. Their economic links with their former colonial masters could not be severed overnight. They changed from 'passives' into 'dependents'. The hierarchy of the international system was not materially affected by the decolonisation.

The system is in constant motion, as history shows. For that reason I will not venture to classify the nations. Besides, any classification would vary according to the criterion chosen. If we take military independence as a yardstick, Western Europe obviously falls under the us. If we take Cox's yardstick of the extent to which external trade relations are determined independently, Western Europe and the usa have to be granted equal rank. In a certain sense the top layers of the hierarchy form a coherent group of countries which inevitably show

140

marked differences on various points, and also rival each other in many respects, but which nevertheless on broader issues have a kind of common understanding in regard to their joint (top) position vis-à-vis the rest of the world.

Such a common understanding is even perceptible between the tops of the capitalist and the communist hierarchic systems, which under pressure of the balance of terror respect each other's spheres of influence[4]. This respect, however, is limited to the spheres of influence in the upper strata of their systems, where the boundaries between the two are sharply drawn. In the lower regions the demarcations are less sharp and they fluctuate. Imperialist rivalry between the two systems occurs on the territory of the Third World, so it is not surprising that representatives of developing countries speak of a 'Russian-American Condominium, being a product of underground agreements, trying to settle their predominance on mankind with formulas of co-existence, sometimes "brightened" with local wars which invariably take place in peripheral countries'.[5]

c. The Centre-Periphery mechanism

Instead of a pyramidal sketch of the international system, made up of different ranks, we can better confine ourselves to a more global characterisation in the spirit of the 'centre-periphery' or the 'metropolis-satellite' thesis. It was by reference to this thesis, that the former secretary general of UNCTAD, Raúl Prebisch regarded the industrialised countries in both the East and the West as the 'Centre', and the developing countries as the 'Periphery' of the world economy.

This Centre-Periphery model can help us better to understand present-day contrasts between the poor and the rich of this world. For this fundamental contrast is manifested not only at an international level (as between rich and poor countries) but just as much within the countries (as between rich and poor sections of the population). The contrast is recognisable in a geographic respect (capital city → provincial town → village) as well as in a social respect (ruling elite → labourers and peasants). In point of fact, society is full of centre-periphery contrasts, which all interlock in such a way that the centre of a lower level always forms part of the periphery of a higher level.

This general pattern which is not, as a rule, interrupted by national boundaries, may be regarded as the constituent mechanism of the international Centre-Periphery model à la Prebisch. The centres (the ruling groups) in the developing countries (the Peripheral countries) are

141

closely linked with the industrialised (Centre) countries, in the sense that the interests of these centre group correspond to a larger extent with the interests of the Centre countries than with the interests of their own domestic periphery. The political leaders in the developing countries, educated in the West and leading a Western style of living, are often completely estranged from their own peoples and cultures. The Centre-Periphery mechanism is then not only upheld and strengthened by specific neo-colonial activities in the political and economic sphere, but equally by the technological and cultural dominance. To many people in the developing countries to develop and to modernise is the same as to adopt Western techniques and values. The distribution of Western literature, films and advertising, the supply of world news through press agencies and broadcasting stations from rich countries, up to and including the presentation of Western parliamentary democracy or the communist party democracy as *the* form of democracy, these all serve to confirm the peripherality of the developing countries.

It is my belief that this picture, which I have borrowed from Galtung[6], goes a long way to explain the present relations between the rich and the poor countries[7]. To my mind, the centre-periphery thesis presents a more truthful picture than, for instance, the one claiming that 'poor and rich co-operate as equal partners'. To assume that this is already the case is to ignore the true relationships, and may constitute an element of camouflage, which may in the long run stand in the way of co-operation on a basis of equality.

For the rest I shall confine myself to the economic conditions in the world, and elucidate the position of dependency of the developing countries in that context.

d. *The developing countries in the world economy*

If we consider the pattern of world trade, the centre-periphery relationship between the rich and the poor countries is clearly discernible. The table below shows that the developing countries' share in total world exports is relatively small and, moreover, is steadily declining.

The combined share of the industrialised countries of East and West in world exports increased in the period from 1960 to 1969 from 78.6 per cent to 82.1 per cent, whilst the developing countries saw their share decrease from 21.4 per cent to 17.9 per cent. The average annual percentage of increase in the developing countries' exports has continually lagged behind the increase in world exports.

142

Table 1. Trend of exports, average annual growth and share in total world exports of several groups of countries from 1960 to 1969 incl. (f.o.b.)

Groups of countries	Period	Value of exports in billions of dollars	Percentage average annual increase	Percentage share of world exports
Capitalist	1960	85.4	–	66.8
industrialised	1966	141.5	8.8	69.6
countries	1967	149.2	5.5	69.6
	1968	167.7	12.3	70.2
	1969	193.0	15.1	71.2
Communist	1960	15.0	–	11.8
industrialised	1966	23.2	7.5	11.4
countries	1967	24.9	7.3	11.6
	1968	27.0	8.3	11.3
	1969	29.5	9.3	10.9
Developing	1960	27.4	–	21.4
countries	1966	38.7	5.9	19.0
	1967	40.3	4.0	18.8
	1968	44.0	9.2	18.4
	1969	48.6	10.5	17.9
World	1960	127.9	–	100.0
	1966	203.4	8.0	100.0
	1967	214.4	5.4	100.0
	1968	238.8	11.3	100.0
	1969	271.1	13.5	100.0

Source: UNCTAD: Review of International Trade and Development, 1969/70 (TD/B/ 309, 7 Aug. 1970, Part One, Annex table I).

The following table shows how between 1960 and 1969 international trade has further concentrated itself in the group of industrialised countries.

During this period, exports within the group of industrialised countries increased by no less than 134 per cent, whereas exports from the developing to the industrialised countries advanced by 83 per cent, and exports from the industrialised to the developing countries by only 79 per cent.[8]

Table 2. Origin and destination of exports between industrial centres and peripheral countries (in billions of $ f.o.b.) in 1960 and 1969

to: from:	year	Cap./Commun. industr. countries	Developing countries	World*
Cap./Commun. industr. countries	1960 1969	76.8 ⎱ 180.0 ⎰ + 134%	23.1 ⎱ 41.3 ⎰ + 79%	100.4 222.5
Developing countries	1960 1969	21.0 ⎱ 38.5 ⎰ + 83%	6.1 ⎱ 9.7 ⎰ + 59%	27.4 48.6
World	1960 1969	97.8 218.4	29.1 51.1	127.9 ⎱ 271.1 ⎰ + 112%

Source: UNCTAD, ditto (derived from Annex table I).

Note: * This column includes a few exports whose destinations could not be ascertained.

Mutual trade between the developing countries lagged behind even more, increasing by only 59 per cent. The increasing peripherality of the developing countries is very obvious from this. Relatively, the industrialised countries are exporting increasingly less to and importing increasingly less from the developing countries. As against this, the developing countries' exports to and imports from the industrialised countries are increasing relatively more sharply than their mutual imports and exports. In table 3 the destinations of the developing countries' exports are set out once again, now in percentages of their total exports.

Table 3. Destinations of exports from the developing countries in percentages of their total exports, in 1960 and 1969

	year	Capitalist industr. countries	Communist industr. countries	Developing countries	World
Developing countries	1960 1969	72.6 74.4	4.7 5.4	22.7 20.2	100.0 100.0

Source: UNCTAD, ditto (derived from Annex table I).

As table 3 shows, the developing countries are becoming increasingly dependent on their markets in the industrialised countries. According

144

to table 4, the same applies to their dependence on the industrialised countries as suppliers of their imports; the only difference being that the communist countries appear to have taken over from the capitalist industrialised countries a small proportion of the orders from the developing countries.

Table 4. Origin of the developing countries' imports in percentages of their total imports, in 1960 and 1969

	year	Capitalist industr. countries	Communist industr. countries	Developing countries	World
Developing	1960	74.8	4.4	20.8	100.0
countries	1969	73.5	7.5	19.0	100.0

Source: UNCTAD, ditto (derived from Annex table I).

Summarising, the following two conclusions are warranted:
1. To the industrialised countries the developing countries are *steadily decreasing* in importance, both as customers and as suppliers.
2. To the developing countries the industrialised countries are *steadily increasing* in importance, both as customers and as suppliers.

The answer to the question why the developing countries are faring so badly in world trade is a pretty obvious one: because they are under-developed! At the root of underdevelopment lies a complex of causes, which we cannot go into in this context. One important factor, however, are the external relations: the economies of the poor countries are extremely vulnerable owing to their excessive dependence on events and developments abroad. As a result of the colonial-style division of labour, their exports – even today – are still very one-sided in compo-sition: more than 84 per cent consist of primary products (agricultural and mining products in crude unprocessed form). The proportion of industrial products, though growing (1960: 9%, 1968: almost 16%), is still terribly small.

Trade in primary products suffers from a number of disadvantages that do not apply to industrial products: (1) the demand for them is rising slowly in relation to the rise in income (low income elasticity); (2) prices of primary products fluctuate sharply in consequence of in-flexibility on the supply and the demand side (low price elasticity). We might call these the natural causes of the deterioration in the trading position of the developing countries. Unfortunately, these causes are not the only ones. They are augmented and aggravated by artificial causes springing from the trading and production policies of the Centre countries, which – as we have seen in the preceding tables – constitute the principal markets of the developing countries. Here I will briefly mention a few points which will be elaborated on in the next chapter, concerning the EEC: (1) the heavily subsidised and protectionist agricultural policy of the rich countries, which cuts down the markets of the developing countries and gets rid of the surpluses on the world market, thereby depressing the prices; (2) synthetic substitutes, the fruits of diligent laboratory research, which oust the natural products from the market; (3) mechanisation and automation in industry, which enable more efficient use to be made of raw materials, thereby reducing their demand; (4) excise and other duties levied on tropical produce; (5) import tariffs and quantitative import restrictions, some of which are directed especially against products from the developing countries; (6) the antiprocessing trend in import duties, which discriminate against raw material processing in the developing countries.

This multiplicity of causes is responsible for the picture we have gleaned from the preceding tables. To this may be added the fact that the developing countries have a growing structural deficit in their balance of trade, caused among other things by the deteriorating terms of trade of their export products.[9] This means that for the imports they need, the developing countries have to supply relatively more and more exports.

In the foregoing I have outlined the structural facts and their causes which – I trust – will have served to demonstrate the (growing) peripherality of the developing countries in the system of world trade. In doing so I have, however, dealt with only a part of the centre-periphery structure of the world economy. Let me conclude this paragraph with an enumeration of the other elements that play a part in this. Owing to limitations of space and in some cases a lack of adequate data, this enumeration will have to be brief. Its sole purpose is further to illustrate the centre-periphery structure of the whole and the position of dependence of the developing countries.

1. *Private investment* emanating from the industrialised countries, notably by the multinational corporations, spread a network of economic interests over the capitalist part of the world. 'Called to act in Latin America with a series of privileges, away from the control of American anti-trust legislation and with the politico-military support

of the government, the large American corporations necessarily will transform themselves into superpowers in any country of the region. Since the corporations handle a large number of the basic decisions concerning investment orientation, the location of economic activities, the orientation of technology, the financing of research, and the degree of integration of regional economies, it is perfectly obvious that the decision-making centres represented by the existing national governments will increasingly be relegated to positions of secondary importance.'[10]

Although the need for foreign capital investment, technology and management know-how is great in many developing countries,[11] there has been evidence in recent years of growing resistance to the practices of the international business world.

The five countries of the Andes market recently concluded an agreement covering a joint policy on foreign capital investment; one of the aims being to subordinate foreign capital to national development planning, to reduce dependence on foreign manipulations, and to further industrialisation by ensuring that the bulk of profits is reinvested locally.[12] As for this latter point, the figures of transferred profits, not only from Latin America, are spectacular. In the period from 1950 to 1965 the amount returned to the US as investment income from the developing countries was $ 25,600 million, whilst in the same period only $ 9000 million went out of the US as new direct investment in the developing countries.[13] I have no figures available concerning non-American industry, but there is little reason for assuming that these will be very different. The 'Japan Economic Journal' recently expressed concern about the increasingly defensive attitude the developing countries are adopting towards capital investment by Japanese entrepreneurs.[14]

Besides investment in the productive sectors, mention should also be made of the penetration of Western banks in many developing countries. Branches are to be found in all the larger towns. Through their activities they control a part of domestic savings in such countries, thereby influencing the circulation of money. Also for insurance the developing countries are largely dependent on private insurance companies in the rich countries. At the UNCTAD negotiations they complained about foreign exchange losses as a result of the drain of insurance and reinsurance premiums.

All these private activities can only be regarded as means of perpetuating and sharpening the Centre-Periphery contrast. The developing countries are frequently forced to submit to the decision-making structure of multinational corporations, and this 'destroys any illusion about the autonomy of the various governments in the Third World'.[15]

2. A glance at the *international transport system* likewise produces evidence of the position of dependence of the developing countries. International shipping, for example, is mainly in the hands of Western shipping companies which are firmly entrenched in international cartels, known as 'liner conferences'. Whereas in 1968 the developing countries supplied more than 63 per cent of the total world cargo, they own but 7 per cent of total shipping tonnage (if we exclude Liberia and Panama, because the large fleets registered in these countries are owned by foreign companies).[16]

A general complaint is that the shipping line services definitely do not favour the developing countries; both as regards the opening up of new markets, and for connections between individual developing countries they are at a disadvantage. Moreover, the freight rates are too high, which means loss of foreign currency, and they operate in a discriminating manner.

The world's airline connections also reflect the Centre-Periphery structure of the world economy. 'The airline network has served mainly to link the nations of a high rank.' 'Naturally, with their powerful position in international air traffic, the major Western companies are a dominant force in IATA'.[17]

3. Not without justification many people want the international organisations, notably the United Nations and its associated functional bodies, to play a leading role in bringing about more just conditions in the world. The hopes of the developing countries are based on that. At the same time, however, we must not close our eyes to the fact that in many respects the UN are considered incompetent by the super powers. The elbow room these international organisations are allowed is never very generous, and occasionally limits are imposed on it by the interests of the permanent members of the Security Council. In the economic sphere special attention should be focused on the World Bank and the International Monetary Fund, in which the contribution and the proportion of votes are determined by the economic importance of the member states. A consequence of this is that their general policy lines reflect the economic views of the industrialised countries. 'In the conflicts which arise between local and foreign interests, both the World Bank and IMF have, since their inception, sided . . . with the foreign investors'.[18]

148

The dominant role in the international monetary system of the 'Group of Ten' (US, UK, Japan, Canada, Sweden and the five most important EEC countries) and the status of the dollar and sterling as international reserve currencies, are an indication of the strong centre position of the Western nations in this area.[19]

4. At the end of this summary attention should be drawn to that part of international aid to the poor countries, which does not really deserve being called 'aid'. I have in mind the loans on (too) onerous terms which, together with the export credits, caused the total debt position of the developing countries in 1969, according to an estimate by the World Bank, to rise to $ 60,000 m., and brought the interest and repayment commitments in that year to some $ 5.300 m.[20] Mention should also be made here of the practice followed by all donor countries of tying the bilateral financial aid to spending in the country furnishing the capital, as a result of which the effective use of this aid is sometimes much less than the amount of aid would suggest (higher prices and loss to potential suppliers in the receiving country or in other developing countries).[21]

II. THE EEC AS PART OF THE CENTRE

Against the background of the picture of the hierarchic international system provided in the preceding paragraphs, I now propose to examine the economic importance of the European Economic Community to the developing countries.

a. The EEC as trading partner of the developing countries

The six EEC countries combined form the largest market for the developing countries. In the following table some figures of exports in 1968 are compared.

Table 5. Exports from developing countries to various industrialised countries in 1968 (in billions of dollars f.o.b.)

	EEC	UK	USA	Eastern Europe	Japan
Developing countries[a]	10.71	4.23	8.40	1.91	4.44

a. excluding China, Mongolia, North Korea and North Vietnam.
Source: UN Statistical Yearbook, 1969.

The importance of the EEC in this respect becomes even more evident if we split up the developing countries by area. The following table indicates the destinations of exports from the various developing countries in percentages of the total exports of the area in question.

Table 6. Destinations of exports from the developing countries by areas (in billions of $ and in percentages of their total exports) in 1965

from:	to:	world bill. $	%	USA & Canada	Western Europe total	EEC	UK	Japan	Other ind.c.	Commun. ind.c.	Developing countriesa
North Africa		2.89 =	100	2	76	60	9	1	–	13	6(2)
Rest of Africa		5.02 =	100	11	65	38	21	3	2	4	12(7)
Middle East		6.46 =	100	7	48	28	12	14	5	2	21(8)
Rest of Asia		9.31 =	100	19	25	11	10	13	4	8	31(24)
Latin America		11.17 =	100	34	33	20	6	5	–	8	19(10)
Rest of devel.c.b		1.87 =	100	40	36	18	16	3	3	–	15(6)
total dev.c.		36.72 =	100	20	41	25	11	8	3	7	21

a. The figure in brackets represents the intra trade of the area in question.
b. Consists mainly of the islands in the Caribbean and the Pacific.
Source: M. Z. Cutajar/A. Franks: The Less Developed Countries in World Trade, Table 5, p. 24.

This table reflects the limited distribution of most of the developing countries' exports. In 1965 the EEC formed the largest market for the African countries and the Middle East. Especially North Africa's heavy concentration on the EEC is noticeable, in sharp contrast with this area's trade with other developing areas. In that year the EEC was also an important trading partner for the Latin American countries; together with the other West European countries it was in fact equal to the North American market. For the developing countries as a whole about a quarter of their exports was going to the EEC in 1965.

If we now consider these trade relations from the angle of the EEC, we arrive at the same picture as the one before in regard to the entire group of industrialised countries, viz.: the developing countries are becoming less important to the EEC, both as a market and as a supplier of imports. In the period from 1960-1968 the EEC's total exports increased by no less than *114* per cent, whereas EEC exports to the developing countries went up by only *38* per cent. The same goes for EEC imports: total imports in this period advanced by *111* per cent;

imports from the developing countries by about *69* per cent.

We may wonder whether the EEC, besides being the biggest market for the combined developing countries (as is clear from tables 5 and 6) is also the fastest growing market. Apparently it is not. During the period from 1960 to 1968 the communist industrialised nations' imports from the developing countries showed the biggest advance, viz. by 81.1 per cent. All the same, the growth in the EEC's imports from the developing countries did compare favourably with that of the capitalist industrialised countries as a whole, although the difference was small, viz. 68.5 and 65.5 per cent respectively. In considering this latter comparison, one should really allow for the fact that the EEC's total imports in this period increased more rapidly (by 111 per cent) than those of the capitalist industrialised countries (100 per cent). A better yardstick for comparison is the decline in the developing countries' exports' share of the total imports by both groups of countries. In the 1960-1968 period the EEC's share dropped from 22 to 17.9 per cent[22], and that of the capitalist industrialised countries from 23.8 to 19.7 per cent. In both cases the decline is 4.1 per cent. From this we may conclude that the decline in the importance of the developing countries as suppliers of the EEC's imports was just as rapid as for the capitalist industrialised countries as a whole. But also: that the developing countries supply a smaller proportion of the EEC's imports than of the combined capitalist industrialised countries' imports. For the purpose of comparison some figures of other industrialised countries are given here; all relating to the developing countries' share in their imports in 1968: USA 26.2%, UK 25.1%, Japan 40.7% and the East European countries only 8.3%. A noticeable development is that the developing countries' share in imports by the communist industrialised countries shows a slight advance, viz. from 8.1 per cent in 1960 to 9.4 per cent in 1969, whereas in respect of all the capitalist industrialised countries this share is declining.

From which developing areas the EEC's imports originated, and what shifts have occurred in the last decade may be seen in the following table:

Table 7. EEC imports from the developing countries in 1960 and 1968 in millions of dollars and in percentages of the total

	1960 $m	%	1968 $m	%
AASM	950	15.2	1,467	14.0
Rest of Africa	1,400	22.4	2,893	27.5
Middle East	1,280	20.5	2,510	24.0
South and East Asia	845	13.5	1.050	10.0
Latin America	1,580	25.3	2,340	22.3
Others	170	3.1	230	2.2
Total developing countries	6,225	100.0	10,490	100.0

Source: E. Pearse/R. Kahn: The White Tribes of Europe (London 1970), p. 9.

It is evident that during this period both the Rest of Africa and the Middle East were able roughly to double their exports to the EEC, and that in consequence the other developing countries, including the Associated African States and Madagascar (AASM), saw their share in these exports decline. The increases recorded by the Rest of Africa and the Middle East are mainly due to EEC imports of oil from Libya, Algeria and the oil countries of the Middle East. The East African Community (Kenya, Tanzania and Uganda) scarcely counts in the Rest of Africa's share.

These two areas of rapid increase are followed in order of largest increase in exports to the EEC by: the AASM, Latin America and Asia. Throughout the 1960-68 period the AASM's exports to the EEC increased by some 54 per cent, whilst Latin America rose by 48 per cent. Only a year earlier it was the other way round: Latin American exports to the EEC in the 1960-67 period advanced by about 50 per cent, whilst AASM exports, despite their preferential treatment under the association agreement, did not manage more than a 37 per cent increase. There were even years when AASM exports to the EEC declined, absolutely speaking (between 1960 and 62 and between 1966 and 67). Since 1967, however, these exports increased substantially, from 1968 to 1969 by no less than 17 per cent, so it seems that the preferential treatment is at last bearing some fruit.

It is interesting to note, incidentally, that whereas AASM exports to the EEC during the period from 1960-1967 advanced by more than 56 percent, total AASM exports to both industrialised and developing countries grew by more than 72 per cent. This suggests that the AASM are gradually reducing their unilateral dependence on the EEC market (in 1960 still 67 per cent, reduced to 60.7 per cent by 1967).[23]

152

The main findings in the foregoing were, therefore:
- that the EEC constitutes the biggest market for the combined developing countries (for the African countries it is indeed excessively large), but that it is not the fastest growing market;
- that the developing countries are declining in importance as trading partners of the EEC and of the other capitalist industrialised countries (not of the communist industrialised countries), but that their share in the EEC's trade is smaller than in that of the other capitalist industrialised countries;
- that the oil-producing countries account for a large share of the rise in EEC imports from the developing countries, and
- that the AASM are reducing their dependence on the EEC market.

b. *Trading, production and association policy of the EEC*

Having examined the general trend of trade relations between the EEC and the developing countries, let us now consider what (EEC) policy lies at the root of this trend. We are concerned with three main elements: the policies governing imports, agriculture and association.

One of the aims of the Treaty of Rome was to establish a *Common External Tariff* (CET). This was set at the average of the tariffs of the individual member states, and entailed an increase for Western Germany and the Benelux, and a reduction in the French and Italian tariffs. In operation since July 1968, this CET is on average lower than the tariffs of the other important industrialised countries. In the following table these tariffs are compared, special attention being directed to the noticeable difference between the tariffs on total imports of industrial products and those on imports of industrial products from the developing countries only.

Table 8. Average nominal and effective tariffs on imported industrial products in a number of industrialised countries (in percentages)[a]

Countries	Average tariffs on total industrial imports		Average tariffs on industrial imports from developing countries	
	nominal	*effective*[b]	*nominal*	*effective*[b]
USA	6.8	11.6	12.4	23.9
UK	9.1	16.0	14.1	27.6
EEC	6.6	11.1	9.4	16.9
Sweden	3.8	6.7	6.6	14.6
Japan	9.4	16.4	11.7	20.2
All industrialised countries	6.5	11.1	11.8	22.6

a. All tariffs taken after implementation of Kennedy Round reductions.
b. See note 24.

Source: UNCTAD: The effects of the Kennedy Round on the exports of processed goods from developing countries, by Bela Balassa (TD/69, Febr. '68).

This table tells us two things about the average tariffs of the industrialised countries mentioned: (A) That the tariff barriers against industrial products from developing countries are considerably higher than those against products from industrialised countries. This discrimination against the developing countries is the result of the range of tariff negotiations the rich countries have conducted in recent years within the framework of the GATT, when they invariably paid more attention to reducing tariffs relating to their mutual trade than to the remaining tariffs. Even after the Kennedy Round (concluded in 1967), Professor Bela Balassa observed '. . . the continuation of a tendency for tariffs on goods which are traded chiefly among industrial countries to be reduced more than tariffs on imports from developing areas'.

At all events, compared with the other countries mentioned, the Swedish tariffs turn out to be the lowest, followed by the CET of the EEC. (B) That the tariffs of all the countries referred to are characterised by an anti-processing tendency, viz. that products that have undergone a further degree of processing carry a higher tariff than less processed products. This is indicated by the average effective tariff.[24]

Comparison of the differences between the nominal and the effective tariffs on both groups of industrial products shows, moreover, that the effective protection against products from the developing countries is higher than that against products from the developing countries.

It should be noted that the figures in table 8 relate to the average of the current tariffs on industrial products. In addition, the tariffs on processed agricultural products sometimes show excessively high effective protection, as illustrated by the following examples: The nominal tariff on cocoa beans is 3.2 per cent, but that on cocoa powder and cocoa butter is 18.2 per cent. The 15 per cent difference expressed as a percentage of the added value of cocoa beans made into powder or butter results in an effective tariff of no less than 126.6 per cent! There is no EEC tariff on groundnuts, but groundnut oil is subject to a nominal tariff of 7.5 per cent. Calculated in the same way, this results in an effective tariff of 92.5 per cent. Copra again carries no tariff, but coconut oil a 10 per cent tariff; effective tariff 85.4 per cent. There are many more products against the processing of which in the producing country the CET discriminates.[25] The developing countries associated

154

with the EEC are exempt from the CET, but I shall revert to this at a later stage.

Besides the tariff restrictions on imports, the EEC – like the other industrialised countries also operates *quantitative import restrictions,* on which there is not yet a common policy, however. Under the Long Term Arrangement on Cotton Textiles all EEC countries apply quotas on imports of manufactured cotton textiles; the object being to protect their domestic textile industries against competition from (mainly) Japan and a number of developing countries (including India, Pakistan, Mexico, Hong Kong, Colombia and the UAR).

In addition, France applies import quotas to canned fish, tobacco products, leather, manufactures of jute and coconut fibre and to sports gear. Italy does the same with tobacco products, Western Germany with manufactures of jute and coconut fibre, leather, woollen yarns, woven fabrics and clothing.[26]

In the EEC countries there also exist *excise* and other *consumption duties* on products from the developing countries such as coffee, tea and cocoa. Such duties are sometimes excessive in relation to the import price, so a reduction could mean rising consumption and a bigger market for the developing countries in question. Moreover, the differentials as between the member countries are so great that a recent symposium in Brussels came to the conclusion '... that if trading margins and taxes were all brought into line with the lowest levels in the Community, sums at least equal to the value of the Community's imports of these products could be released, with no rise in the price to the consumer.'[27]

Generally trade restrictions are the result of certain domestic production circumstances which make it necessary to bar foreign competition. This is particularly evident in agriculture, which is experiencing difficulties in most industrialised countries. We must now consider some of the consequences of the *Common Agricultural Policy* (CAP) of the European Community for the export position of the developing countries.[28]

The CAP has resulted in agricultural prices which in comparison to prices in neighbouring agricultural areas, not to mention the world market price level, are on the high side.

In order to maintain these prices so as to provide farmers with a reasonable income, a system of variable and fixed import levies and export subsidies has been devised which – with a few exceptions – sets the EEC market completely apart from the outside world. Supplemented by a market intervention mechanism and a whole range of specific

155

measures such as premiums, interest subsidies, information and guidance, etc., this system, aided by the enormous technological advances in agriculture, has resulted in a sharp rise in production on the entire (green) front. In the case of some products this growth in production has actually outstripped the increase in consumption. Expressing production as a percentage of consumption gives us the degree of self sufficiency. Some relevant data are combined in the table below.

Table 9. Degree of the EEC's self sufficiency in a number of agricultural products and food (in percentages)

products	1962/63 1963/64	1964/65	1965/66	1966/67	1967/68
Wheat	99.5	105.7	110.0	96.0	112.5
Coarse grains	77.1	74.6	70.9	72.0	78.6
Rice (hulled)	79.0	79.0	59.9	79.8	100.8
White sugar	98.7	119.7	104.1	98.7	104.6
Butter	99.5	102.0	101.7	108.8	111.1
Oils and fats	38.5	37.2	36.8	36.3	41.8
Beef	90.3	86.4	84.4	86.8	88.8

Source: Recommendations by the Commission to the Council regarding the applications for entry of the UK, Ireland, Denmark and Norway (1 Oct. 1969), p. 88.

More recent estimates suggest that self sufficiency in coarse grains has meanwhile risen further, and that self-sufficiency in sugar in the 1970/71 season has actually reached 116 per cent.

The following table illustrates how this policy, which leads to a sharp rise in production, seriously hampers the developing countries in their exports to the EEC.

Table 10. Net imports by the EEC of products coming under the Common Agricultural Policy in 1963/64 and in 1968 (in $ m.)

Origin	1963/64	1968	changes in %
World	2,436	2,337	— 4%
USA	830	973	+ 18%
Developing countries	1,227	906	— 26%

Source: A. Zeller: L'Imbroglio Agricole du Marché Commun (1970), p. 105.

It will be seen that total imports of CAP products have declined. The most surprising development is that imports from the developing countries have fallen by 26 per cent, whereas those from the USA have increased by 18 per cent. This latter increase is due among other things to the rapid rise in imports of maize and oleagenous seeds and animal foodstuffs made from them (soya beans and soya meal).[29] The EEC does not impose import levies on oil seeds. The developing countries might also have benefited from this, if they had not had to compete with subsidised exports from the US. The vegetable oils and fats sector demonstrates, incidentally, that it is not only production restrictions that are capable of hampering trade, but that the import policy of the importing countries is also a major factor. According to a recently published SER report, the developing countries' declining share in the international trade in vegetable oils and fats is mainly attributable to the high level of support given to production in the industrialised countries.[30] Mrs. 't Hooft-Welvaars has the following to say about this: 'One cannot help thinking that the support level of vegetable oils and fats is aimed at making the EEC increasingly self supporting in those areas where its own production does not yet cover consumption'.[31]

Especially colza and sunflowerseed production are increasing at an enormous rate in the EEC. 'On top of that', says the aforementioned SER report, 'under the influence of the support policy, animal fats (butter) produced in the EEC are increasingly competing in the world market with vegetable fats, likewise to the detriment of the developing countries' exports'.[32]

The best-known example of the injuriousness of European agricultural policy to the developing countries is that of sugar beet production. Sugar is the only product under the CAP, the production of which cannot be expanded limitlessly by the individual producer, but these limits have been fixed well beyond the EEC's own requirements. The producers receive various prices: production up to 105 per cent of EEC consumption in 1968 (the basic quota) qualifies for the 'fat' price; the 'semi-fat' price applies to 105-135 per cent, whilst for production beyond that level the farmer receives no more than the world market price which fluctuates around one quarter of the 'fat' EEC price. This policy is clearly aimed at surpluses, surpluses which have subsequently to be got rid of at great cost (export drawbacks, denaturing premiums, etc., which amounted to around Dfl. 250 m. in 1968 and some Dfl. 360 m. in 1969 in the Community). Roughly 70 per cent was exported and 30 per cent processed into fodder. For the 1970/71 season the sugar surplus is estimated at about 1 m. tons.[33]

This is the policy which in 1968 was responsible for the EEC's refusal to join the International Sugar Agreement (ISA) concluded in that year. The export quota offered to the EEC in the first instance was 300,000 tons, but the EEC demanded a quota of no less than 1.2 m. tons, a quantity never reached in the preceding years (the average quantity available for export from 1961 to 1967 was 386,000 tons).[34] This confirms the prior intention not to participate in the export quotas within the framework of the ISA. The EEC preferred to go it alone, aiming at an increased surplus production equalling 17 per cent of consumption, even though the participating exporting countries agreed to limit their offer, so as to stabilise the world sugar market. This EEC policy is partly responsible for the ISA's failure to realise this aim, to the detriment of the cane sugar-exporting developing countries.[35]

The last subject to be dealt with in this paragraph is the *association policy* of the Community. For special categories of developing countries exceptions have been made to the rules of the Common External Tariff (CET) and the Common Agricultural Policy (CAP). France's overseas territories (Départements d'Outre Mer – DOM), for example, are considered to belong to the EEC, and their products are treated as indigenous production (mainly sugar and bananas).

Then there is the category of the dependent developing countries, which are indicated as Territoires d'Outre Mer (TOM), such as Surinam and the Netherlands Antilles and a number of French territories such as French Somaliland and various islands in the Atlantic, the Pacific and the Indian Ocean. These TOM are exempt from the CET, but not from the import levies connected with the CAP. Their principal exports are: copra, rice, spices, some oils and – from New Caledonia – nickel.

The association with the former African colonies of France, Belgium and Italy, designated the Associated African States and Madagascar (AASM) is similar in broad lines to that with TOM.

The first arrangement with AASM after it had become independent was made within the context of the Yaoundé Convention, which became effective in 1964 and had a 5-year term. In 1969 the negotiations for extending the association were concluded, and recently – after a protracted period of ratification – Yaoundé II became effective (valid until 31 Jan. 1975).

The system of preferences under the Yaoundé association (exemption from the Common External Tariff, but not from the levies of the Common Agricultural Policy) is based on the principle of reciprocity, i.e., that in return EEC products can be imported into the AASM tariff free. Fiscal import duties, however, may be maintained. By way of general exception to this rule of reciprocity the AASM may, after prior consultation with the EEC, impose non-discriminating customs duties on EEC products for reasons of a budgetary, protective or development nature. This exception clause also exists in regard to mutually agreed

158

abolition of quantitative import restrictions. During the negotiations in 1969 the AASM pressed for more facilities for taking measures to safeguard their nascent industries. These facilities are extended in scope and better formulated in the new Yaoundé agreement. The AASM also asked for abolition of the import restrictions on CAP products (processed and unprocessed) and abolition of the consumer taxes on tropical products, but on these points they did not get their own way with the EEC.[36]

Besides the trade regulations in the associations with the AASM and the TOM, special provisions have been made for furnishing financial and technical aid via the European Development Fund (EDF). (Yaoundé II also relates to EDF III). In the first and second association arrangements this aid was partly meant as compensation for the disappearance of the former French 'surprise' system for the CFA countries (Communauté Financière Africaine, formed by 14 former French colonies). EDF III has a budget of $ 900 m., whilst a further $ 100 m. is made available by the European Investment Bank (EIB). The bulk of this fund will be made available in the form of gifts ($ 810 m.), the balance as loans on special terms ($ 90 m.). Allocation among the receiving countries is as follows: AASM $ 918 m. and DOM and TOM $ 82 m.

A comparison between the first and second EDF in regard to allocations to the various countries of the tenders and the supply of goods and technical aid produces the following picture:

Table 11. Comparison between 1st and 2nd EDF allocations (position as at 31-12-'69) in $ m.

Countries	1st EDF		2nd EDF	
	amount	%	amount	%
Belgium	17.28	3.81	28.18	8.87
W. Germany	29.16	6.43	74.46	23.45
France	197.61	43.55	116.64	36.73
Italy	62.19	13.70	34.10	10.74
Luxembourg	1.42	0.31	1.16	0.37
Netherlands	22.82	5.03	10.21	3.21
AASM/DOM/TOM	122.94	27.09	52.37	16.49
Third countries	0.38	0.08	0.46	0.14
Total	453.80	100.00	317.58	100.00

Source: Parliamentary Paper 10 606, session 1969/70, memorandum relating to the Report, No. 6, Appendix II.

It appears that France continues to be the principal supplier (and profiteer) of EDF activities, although her share is on the decline, mainly in favour of W. Germany. A remarkable feature, however, which to my mind conflicts with the real object of the development contributions, is the fall, both absolute and relative, in the investment projects in the developing countries themselves.[37] Evidently not enough is being done to encourage these countries' local industries. In the former French territories it has so far been mainly the local French corporations that have carried out the EDF projects. It is well known that the French are not very keen on sharing their strong sphere of influence in Africa with the other member states '. . . and from the outset, they seized the predominant role in Community policy and the Commission staff in relations with African associates'.[38]

In this connection special mention should be made of the position of extreme dependence of the 14 CFA countries referred to earlier. The currency of these countries, the CFA franc, is not covered by their own stocks of gold and foreign currency, and can be freely exchanged for the French franc. All their foreign payments are made via France, and the balances are kept with the French treasury. This gives France a controlling influence on the monetary and trading policies of these countries. Even after the 1967 agreements they require prior authorisation by France for dealings in foreign securities and gold, and for obtaining loans outside the franc zone. 'So in effect the African currencies remain tied to the French franc.'[39]

The special relations of the EEC with developing countries have not remained limited to the aforementioned groups. With Nigeria an association agreement was signed in 1968, consisting only of trade regulations and without EDF aid, which never became effective, however. With the countries of the East African Community (Kenya-Tanzania and Uganda) negotiations were renewed in 1969, after an association agreement had already been concluded in 1968. The East African states would have liked to see the agreement extended to cover financial and technical aid, on the lines of the Yaoundé association, but the EEC would not hear of this. The Treaty of Arusha in September '69 again related exclusively to trade. With the exception of coffee, cloves and canned pineapple, which are subject to some restrictions, the products of the East African countries can enter the EEC entirely duty free. In regard to the principle of reciprocity the negotiations with these three countries had run into considerable difficulties. However, the EEC insisted on at least a symbolic gesture in return, so as not to be confronted subsequently with the same opposition on the part of the

160

AASM.[40] The reversed preferences relate to only 59 products, together accounting for about 1/6 of EEC exports to East Africa.

The three North African countries Algeria, Tunisia and Morocco, even after gaining independence, retained special trading preferences on the French market. For Tunisia and Morocco the EEC Treaty featured the 'Morocco Protocol', whilst Algeria at that time was still part of France. After gaining independence, Algeria did not join the Yaoundé Association, so in 1965 four of the EEC countries (Italy and Benelux) were able to seize on the French boycott in the EEC as a reason for not allowing further tariff reductions on Algerian produce. In 1970 the Algerian government officially announced that it desired a new arrangement.

In 1967 the preferential treatment of Tunisia and Morocco on the French market was changed for the greater part into an association agreement with the EEC. Under this agreement practically all the industrial products of these two countries are exported duty-free to the Community. Mineral oil is subject to quantitative restrictions. Fruit and vegetables enjoy a preference equal to 80 per cent of the Common External Tariff (CET). Morocco and Tunisia, in return grant EEC products preferences of 25 per cent and 70 per cent respectively.

Even outside the African continent the EEC has established special relations with developing countries. A special agreement with Turkey which became operative in 1964 provides for association in three phases, possibly leading to membership of the Community in the future. The negotiations for the agreement to enter upon its second phase were concluded in 1970, but still have to be ratified. They provide for immediate abolition of the EEC tariffs and quantitative restrictions (with a special arrangement for textile and mineral oil products and preferences for 90 per cent of Turkish agricultural products). In reciprocation Turkey is required only to abolish gradually its duties on EEC imports. In addition, Turkey will receive $ 195 m. in 'soft' loans over a periode of 5½ years.

With Israel an agreement was concluded in 1964, granting that country selective preferences. In 1970 a fresh preferential agreement was entered into, granting Israel tariff reductions on more than 85 per cent of its industrial exports and about 80 per cent of its agrarian exports to the EEC. Israel, on its part, applies tariff cuts to more than half its imports from the EEC. These reversed preferences are being implemented in stages. There are those that advocate the setting up of a complete free-trade zone with Israel.[41]

Following a relatively brief period of negotiations a trade agreement

161

with Iran was concluded in 1963[42], based on the most-favoured-nation principle and relating to a few products (incl. woollen carpets, of which Iran is the Community's main supplier). More than 80 per cent of Iranian exports, however, consist of mineral oil, which the Community already imports duty free.

In May 1965 the EEC concluded an agreement with Lebanon, which in addition to trading terms on the most-favoured-nation basis also contained provisions for technical aid. The latter in fact constituted the first form of co-ordinated action in development aid by the Six (albeit not the establishment of a Community policy) in respect of a developing country not belonging to the former colonies of the member states.[43] This technical aid programme, though limited in scope, appears to function. Negotiations are now being conducted with Lebanon concerning a preferential trade agreement.

The same applies to the UAR. An association agreement with Malta became operative on 1st April 1970, which provides for the establishment of a customs union in two stages of 5 years. The possibility of association with Cyprus is being investigated. As regards the further relations in the Mediterranean it should be mentioned that a preferential agreement with Spain has been in operation since October 1970, that a non-preferential agreement with Yugoslavia was concluded in March 1970, and that negotiations are still proceeding with Portugal regarding a form of closer relations or association with the Community. If any special link is established with Portugal in particular, the Community will run the risk of getting involved in that country's colonial policy in Africa. The association with Greece, in operation since 1962, has been more or less in cold storage since the military seized power in 1967, although the provisions of the Treaty of Athens, especially in regard to the regulation of trade, are being carried out. Bilateral agreements have also been concluded with a few developing countries under the Long Term Agreement on Cotton Textiles (India, Pakistan, Taiwan, South Korea and Hong Kong); arrangements have also been made for other textile products.

Lastly, the Latin American nations have been kept on a string ever since the establishment of the EEC. Consultation within contact groups, the drafting of memoranda, and resolutions in the European Parliament have alternated with regularity. However, negotiations have meanwhile been started with Argentina on a non-discriminatory trade agreement, whilst the possibility of an agreement with Uruguay is still being examined.

c. The General Preference System (GPS)

As we have seen earlier on, the special relations between the EEC and the Third World at present cover a fairly considerable number of developing countries (though actually less than 10 per cent of the population of the developing countries). The various agreements differ somewhat in purport and institutional design, which is a result of the 'ad hoc' approach to the external relations with developing countries. Despite several efforts, the Community has not succeeded in plotting an unequivocal common association course. Nobody will deny that the lack of political unity in the Europe of the Six constitutes an obstacle. The need for political vision in the relations with the developing countries has been stressed lately[44] in various quarters, and the elaboration of such a vision is considered all the more urgent now that the Community of the Six is about to be enlarged into a Community of Ten. This latter point will be dealt with more thoroughly in the following chapter. In this paragraph I would like to draw attention to a number of measures by which the Community seeks to demonstrate that it is also doing something for the developing countries not directly connected with it.[45]

In the first place I would mention that during the negotiations in 1969 regarding renewal of the Yaoundé association, the Dutch representatives pressed for a lowering of the CET for some tropical products by way of a gesture to show that 'the interests of non-associated developing countries were also taken into account'. This urging resulted in a slight reduction in the duties on palm oil (of special importance to Indonesia), coffee and cocoa. Tariff cuts were also authorised for a few other, less important, products.[46] At the same time a protocol (Protocol No. 4) was appended to the Yaoundé II agreement, stating that the provisions of the Agreement did not stand in the way of the establishment of a general system of preferences within the framework of the UNCTAD, and did not constitute an obstacle to participation in such a system by the associated states. In the same way, the Netherlands tried to get the reciprocity in the Yaoundé preferences gradually abolished, but this met with vigorous opposition from the French. No doubt influenced by the French attitude, and probably fearing gradual oblivion of the preferences to be granted them by the EEC, even the association countries themselves, paradoxically enough, were not much in favour of abolition of the reciprocity. They maintain that they are attached to this principle because it is indicative of the parity basis of the agreement. Clearly, the centre-periphery mechanism still operates very strongly in these territories.

The intention of these Dutch initiatives was deliberately to lessen and if possible remove those elements in this regional preference agreement, which might be an obstacle to the establishment of a general system of preferences. The principle of reciprocity meets with resistance on the part of several countries, including the US, which has repeatedly stated that it does not wish to grant preferences to those developing countries that discriminate against American exports in their markets.

In the years when the idea of the general, non-reciprocal and non-discriminatory tariff preferences to be granted in favour of all developing countries by all industrialised countries were discussed, these and several other issues seriously hampered agreement at an early stage. The fundamental decision was reached at the time of the second UNCTAD in New Delhi in 1968. In the period that followed, the Special Committee for Preferences set up at the time could make only slow progress with the definitive working out of the agreement in principle. At first the developing countries still hoped that it would be possible for the General Preference System (GPS) to start operating early in 1970. Now we are well into 1971, and the only definite thing at this moment is that the EEC Council of Ministers decided on 30th March last that the GPS chosen by the EEC will become effective on 1st July next.

This follows a tug of war lasting for many months, for it appeared that the GPS methods advocated by the US and the EEC differed so much from each other in conception that it was impossible to institute a uniform GPS. In May 1970 the Council of Ministers of the OECD decided by way of compromise that the two systems could operate side by side, and that at a certain time in the future the possibility of improvement and harmonisation could be examined anew. The GPS proposed by the US, implies complete abolition of tariffs without quantitative restrictions, but with safeguards of a general nature, whilst some vulnerable products such as textiles, footwear, mineral oil and mineral oil derivatives are excluded entirely from the GPS. Lastly, duty-free imports of a limited number of processed agricultural products is permitted.

The EEC-GPS will take the form of complete abolition of duties on semi manufactures and end products up to a certain maximum value of annual imports, which is calculated each year anew for each product on the basis of uniform criteria. This maximum value per product is determined by reference to a basic value, corresponding with actual

164

imports (CIF value) in 1968 into the EEC from all developing countries coming under the GPS (the so-called basic quota). This basic value is increased each year by 5 per cent of the value of the imports from all other countries in the previous year, or in the year for which the most recent data are available (the 'supplementary quota'). It is stipulated that the preferential imports must never be less than those of the preceding year. It is also laid down that one individual developing country will never be able to import duty free more than half of the preferential quota thus calculated. This stipulation is made in order that the weaker developing countries shall also benefit by the preferences, and to ensure that competition against the EEC's own European industry shall not be too great (the 'buffer' clause)[47].

Preferential treatment in respect of cotton textiles is granted only to those developing countries that subscribe to the 'Long Term Arrangement on Cotton Textiles', and those countries that are prepared to accept the provisions of this 'Arrangement' vis-à-vis the EEC. Some preferential rights will also be granted for jute and coconut products. As for agricultural products, in regard to which the developing countries have repeatedly advocated that they should also come under the GPS, the EEC has compiled a list of products to which a preferential tariff cut will apply. In compiling this list the EEC took account of the AASM's interests. These processed agricultural products are not subject to quantitative limits.

The EEC has not yet decided definitively to which countries the GPS will apply eventually. They want to decide this jointly with the other industrialised countries within the context of the OECD. For the time being, however, the EEC-GPS will apply to the countries of the 'Group of 77' (now 91 countries), and to certain dependent territories such as Hong Kong, Macao, Angola and other Portuguese colonies. In respect of this latter category of dependent countries, textiles and footwear are, however, excluded from the GPS.[48] As Cuba, Israel and Taiwan do not belong to the 'Group of 77', they fall outside the GPS for the present. The GPS will be effective for 10 years, initially.

It is not yet possible to assess the effectiveness of the EEC-GPS which becomes operative next July. The initial impression is that it excels in cautiousness. Considering the whole design of the system, the EEC will never be taken by surprise. The annual increase in preferential imports can never be more than 5 per cent of the non-preferential imports during the last year for which data are available. In other words: the supplementary quota is dependent on the volume of non-preferential imports, and can increase only if the latter have risen. As regards the initial rise in preferential imports (i.e. the increase in relation to the situation without preferences), it may be said that this will increase with the share in total imports from countries not coming under the GPS. In other words: the smaller the basic quota in relation to total imports, the greater the supplementary quota of preferential imports. In the case of products for which the developing countries are already competitive and have secured a large share of EEC imports, the rise in preferential imports will be relatively less.

Apart from this, one may well ask whether, in regard to products that are subject to quantitative import restrictions, such as cotton textiles, the preferences granted offer the developing countries in question any great advantage. After all, the volume of imports permitted remains the same as in the situation without preferences. Benefits, for instance, in terms of a higher export yield, arise only in so far as the developing countries can secure higher prices from importers in the EEC.

Also, the choice of 1968 as reference year for the calculations will not give the developing countries much satisfaction, for in that year Latin American exports to the EEC were at an extremely low level; compared with 1967 their value dropped by $ 120 m., whilst from 1968 to 1969 it increased by almost $ 500 m.

A major drawback of the GPS system to be instituted by the EEC is its appalling complexity. The annual calculations of the preferential quotas by product, and the constant attention needed to prevent the quota from being exceeded or one country taking on more than its share, entail the sort of paperwork and red tape with which they may be familiar in Brussels, but which hardly seems suitable to promote trade.

In this connection it should also be remembered that, the developed countries having failed jointly to institute a uniform system of preferences, many of the attractive aspects of a GPS have been lost. Each industrialised country is now applying its own methods. Japan and Austria are working with quantitative maximums, just like the EEC. The other countries are not, but each of them has different products on the list of exceptions, or they operate variable tariff reductions. The GPS is far from being a general system. The unsophisticated exporter in a developing country, who in the past has had quite enough difficulty in mastering the mass of tariff and non-tariff regulations in force all over the world, is certainly not going to find things any easier.

There is just one more comment I wish to make on the new preference system. It does not look as if it could replace the existing limited regional preference systems. In including processed agricultural

166

products, the EEC has deliberately taken into account the interests of the associated states, by restricting this list. There is something to be said for that, for several of the associated countries belong to the category of 'least developed developing countries', which can expect little compensation from a GPS under which they have to share their preferences with other, more developed developing countries. At the same time, however, this means that the regional division into trading blocs, in which the Centre-Periphery mechanism operates more effectively, is not affected for the present. The GPS in the form in which it will operate in the near future, is far from being a radical intervention in the present world trading system. This does not alter the fact that it will be capable of conferring a few advantages here and there, which may be considered as a bonus. All this is on the assumption and in the hope that the other industrialised countries will soon proceed to put their preferences into effect.

III. THE ENLARGEMENT OF THE EUROPEAN COMMUNITY AND THE DEVELOPING COUNTRIES

In the previous chapter we have demonstrated how the Europe of the Six performs its role as a major market for the developing countries. Before passing judgment on this part of the Centre of the world economy in its relations with the Periphery, let me first examine in this chapter what the effects will be of the further integration in the Centre, which is now the focal point of the discussion, viz., the applications for membership of the European Community from the United Kingdom, Ireland, Denmark and Norway. Of these four candidate countries only Britain belongs to the leading nations of the international hierarchic system. Together with the EEC, Britain represents no less than 34 per cent of the total market of the developing countries (in 1968: $ 14,940 m.) and in 1969 it supplied 46.4 per cent of the total gross flow of finance and technical aid of the DAC countries to the developing countries (approx. $ 6,300 m.).

a. *Reorganisation of the special relations*[49]

The former British Empire is now kept together, more or less, within the framework of the Commonwealth (at present comprising 28 states). When in the years between World Wars I and II Britain gradually abolished its traditional free trade policy and instituted tariffs and other import restrictions, an exception was made for the countries and territories that formed part of the Commonwealth. Thus was created the Commonwealth Preference Zone (CPZ), which was consolidated at the Imperial Economic Conference of Ottawa in 1932. The CPZ applies to both industrialised and developing countries in the Commonwealth; the former supplied 20 per cent, the latter 13 per cent of Britain's total imports in 1966. The CPZ also applies to a few non-Commonwealth countries, such as the Republic of Ireland, South Africa, South-West Africa, Western Samoa and Burma; Rhodesia being (temporarily?) excluded from the CPZ. The developing countries which thus have free access to the British market form a not unimportant part of the Third World; if China is discounted, it houses half the population of the developing countries. The industrial products of all other developing countries are subject to the 'Full Tariff', which – as we have seen in table 8 – has an average nominal level of 14.1 per cent, which amounts to an effective average tariff of 27.6 per cent. However, in addition, several important foodstuffs and raw materials such as wheat, mutton and lamb, raw rubber, raw fibres (incl. cotton and jute), metal ores and unworked metal, are imported into the UK duty free.

Trade within the CPZ is as a rule entirely duty free. A few exceptions to this rule are, however, of importance to certain developing countries. They relate to certain processed raw materials (such as fully refined sugar, instant coffee and instant tea) and manufactures (clocks and watches, musical instruments, motor vehicles and goods made of man-made fibres). Further protection of the British processing industry against competition from the 'low-wage countries' is provided by means of restrictive import quotas. These include restrictions on imports of cotton and jute textiles from, inter alia, India, Pakistan and Hong Kong. Imports of sugar are likewise subject to quantitative regulations, but these operate in favour of the respective developing countries, as we shall see later on.

Like the EEC associations, the CPZ is of a reciprocal nature, although a few exceptions are formed by countries which do not grant tariff preferences on British products (incl. Ghana, Nigeria, Kenya, Uganda, Tanzania, Burma, Sierra Leone, Zambia and, for the greater part, Malaysia). According to Cutajar and Franks, there is a noticeable equivalency between the average preferential margins Britains enjoys in the CPZ and those of the CPZ in Britain.[50]

When Britain becomes a member of the European Community, this will probably mean the end of the CPZ in its present form, which cannot fail to have an adverse effect on the trade of the Commonwealth countries. For they will in future be faced with the CET and the CAP of the enlarged Community, and considering the terms of entry Britain will have to accept, the CET and the CAP will not look very different from what they do in the EEC of the Six. Especially for certain tropical products the CET, to protect the interests of the associated states, is quite considerable, in spite of the recent reductions for palm oil, coffee and cocoa. Jamaica and the Windward Isles, for example, sell 96 per cent of their bananas on the British market under preferential treatment. In the absence of special measures they would be subject to a CET of no less than 20 per cent, after Britain's entry. Other Commonwealth developing countries, such as India and Hong Kong, are worried about the CET to which their manufactures will be subject.

Apart from the damage that threatens to result from the application of the CET in Britain, we must also consider the competition with which the traditional suppliers will henceforth be faced on the British market, in the form of products which under the association regime can be freely imported from the present association countries. The Caribbean Commonwealth countries are afraid, not without reason, that their rum will be ousted from the British market by the active and well organised rum producers in the French territories of Martinique, Guadeloupe and Réunion. Of course, the same problems will apply to the countries already associated, if the developing countries of the Commonwealth become associated with the enlarged Community in the wake of Britain's entry. Simple association with only freedom from tariff will in some cases not suffice to protect the interests of traditional suppliers, but will have to be supplemented with guaranteed quotas.

EEC authorities, incidentally, have made it clear that not all Commonwealth developing countries will be eligible for association. In this connection they have referred to the Declaration of Intent accepted in 1963 on the occasion of the Yaoundé Convention I by the Council of Ministers. In this Declaration of Intent the member states declared their willingness to examine with third countries requesting this and whose economic structure and production are comparable with those of the AASM, the possibility of entering into an association or a trading agreement. From a note in the Minutes it appears that the term 'third countries' used in the Declaration of Intent refers especially to the countries of the Commonwealth. Yet in the Recommendations the European Commission sent the Council regarding the applications for membership by the UK, Ireland, Denmark and Norway, a footnote reads: 'States situated in Africa, south of the Sahara, and in the region of the Caribbean Isles'.

Apart from the fact that the Declaration of Intent relates only to a limited number of countries (the Asian Commonwealth countries in particular, are excluded), there is some difference of opinion between France and the other member states in regard to the question whether the Declaration as such should be interpreted as offering the third countries in question the choice between (a) joining the AASM association, (b) their own association agreement, or (c) a non-discriminatory trade agreement, or whether such choice is not intended. France takes the latter view, and that point was emphasised when the Declaration of Intent was confirmed during the Yaoundé II negotiations in 1969.[51]

However that may be, for the Asian Commonwealth developing countries association with the enlarged EEC appears to be out of the question. There may be a chance of a non-preferential trade agreement with the countries that might wish for that, but that could only be discussed after successful conclusion of the negotiations for membership, and not as a part of it.[52] Moreover, EEC circles point to the advantages these countries, possibly even more than the developing countries, will be able to obtain from the General Preference System. Here it should be remembered however, that this GPS is highly restrictive in regard to textile products, which are of great interest to some Asian developing countries, and that it offers no solution for most agricultural products, which are not covered by it. This brings us to the agricultural problems, which are a major factor in the present negotiations.

b. *Effects of agricultural integration*

Until recently, British agricultural policy differed considerably from the CAP in the EEC. Broadly speaking, one might say that the British market for agricultural products was not shielded from the world market in the way the CAP is.[53] On the other hand, the British producer is helped with subsidies, information and guidance, etc., whilst his income is guaranteed by direct price allowances by product (known as deficiency payments). In regard to the latter, the principal difference compared with the EEC system is: In Britain the farmer's income has so far been supplemented by the exchequer, whereas in the EEC this is done by means of the higher market price fixed; in other words: the consumer foots the bill. But even if we include the deficiency payments, the prices of most products in Britain are appreciably lower than in Europe, as is evident from the following table.

170

Table 12. Average prices received by the producers for several agri-cultural products (Dfl. per 100 kg.) in 1966/67

Products	EEC[4]	UK[3]
Wheat	38.46	25.50
Rye	35.30	21.50
Barley	34.19	24.10
Sugar beet[1]	61.54[5]	60.40[6]
(l.w.) beef cattle	246.16[7]	162.70
(l.w.) pigs[2]	266.07[8]	185.30
Milk	35.30[9]	39.10

1. per ton, excl. pulp value
2. the difference in pig prices is, of course, closely connected with the difference in coarse grain prices
3. incl. deficiency payments
4. target prices 1968/69
5. minimum price per ton
6. adjusted for pulp value
7. orientation price
8. basic price slaughtered pigs up to 1 Aug. '68
9. ex farm price

Source: Report of Social & Economic Council No. 11, 1969, p. 14, table 7.

It should be remembered that this is only a snapshot. Meanwhile several prices in the EEC have been increased: wheat and rye by 2%, barley by 4%, milk by 6%, maize by 1% and beef by 6%. The price of sugar will probably go up later in the year.

The intention is that when Britain joins the EEC, these differences will be eliminated, so that there will again be a common price level throughout the enlarged Community. Obviously, such adjustment of prices will encourage increases in production in the UK. The same will happen in Denmark, for there, too, the general level of prices is much lower than in the EEC. Therefore, it is not unreasonable to predict increases in production in the agriculture of the enlarged European Community. In this connection it is important to examine the degree of self sufficiency in the Community of Ten.

Table 13. Comparison between the degree of selfsufficiency of the EEC of Six and the enlarged EEC in 1967/68 (in %)

Products	the Six	the Ten
Wheat	112.5	97.6
Coarse grains	78.6	79.6
Rice (hulled)	100.8	85.9
White sugar	104.6	83.0
Butter	111.1	91.8
Oils and fats	41.8	40.1
Beef	88.8	97.6

Source: the same as table 9.

This comparison demonstrates how splendidly the Six and the Four complement each other in agriculture. In all the products of which the EEC had a surplus in the 1967/68 season, the four candidate countries jointly had a deficit, so that the self-sufficiency degree of the Ten is less than that of the Six. For the present, the enlarged EEC will have no problem of surpluses. This means that there will again be elbow room in the Common Market, and no reason whatsoever for curbing the increases in production to be expected on account of the price adjustments mentioned earlier on.

In summary we may say that we have been able in the foregoing to point to two effects of the agricultural integration as part of the enlargement of the Community, as a result of which Britain's traditional suppliers of agricultural products, which include the developing countries, will see their market share shrink, and in the case of some products even vanish: (1) the price adjustments will induce British and Danish farmers to expand their production, and (2) the EEC surpluses will take over a part of the British market. To these two effects we can add a third (though on account of the limited price elasticity it is likely to be smaller), viz., the fact the higher food prices in Britain and Denmark will have a negative influence on consumption.

It should be pointed out that these adverse effects of the agricultural integration – unlike the consequences of the reorganisation of the special relations of the EEC on the one hand and the UK on the other, relate to the category of developing countries as a whole, at least in so far as they are suppliers of agricultural products that compete with the agriculture of the enlarged Community (this applies to roughly half the agrarian exports of the developing countries). Besides the developing countries there are also a few industrialised countries whose interests on this point are at stake. New Zealand is dependent on the British market for about 90 per cent of its exports of lamb, for roughly the same proportion of its butter exports, and for nearly 80 per cent of its cheese exports. Australia is afraid it will lose part of its market for canned fruit, whilst it will also have to find alternative outlets for its butter. New Zealand, however, is a pressing case, as the figures show. That is why it constitutes one of the issues in the negotiations between Britain and the Six. That also applies to the problem of sugar, to which I will devote the last part of this chapter.

c. *Sugar the touchstone?*

In the preceding chapter I qualified the EEC sugar policy as the best known example of the injuriousness of the CAP to the developing countries. As a result of the agricultural integration this injurious effect now threatens to extend to the UK as well. And this is most regrettable, for it is true to say that Britain's sugar policy is both economically sound and favours a number of developing countries. Economically sound, because Britain's sugar requirements are covered by cheap imports. Favourable for certain developing countries, because within the framework of the Commonwealth Sugar Agreement (CSA) a fixed volume of imports is guaranteed at a price which is generally well above the free world market price (the Negotiated Price Quotas).

The actual position is shown in the following table.

Table 14. Production, consumption and imports of sugar in the UK

	Demand	Supply	Share as a %
	(million tons)		of demand
Home consumption	2.80		100
Home production		0.94	34
Imports: CSA n.p.q.		1.71	61
balance at			
world market prices		0.15	5

Source: AWD Trust, Briefing Paper Sugar (from: Official Trade and Demographic Statistics), p. 3.

From this table it is evident that Britain covers the bulk of its sugar requirements (66%) by imports, and that these are regulated entirely by the CSA. At present the following countries benefit by this CSA: Australia, West Indies and Guiana, British Honduras, East Africa, Mauritius, Swaziland and India. The following data serve to illustrate the importance of sugar to some of these countries.

Table 15. The importance of sugar to come CSA countries

Country	Sugar in % of total exports	Sugar to UK in % of total exports	Employment in sugar production in % of total employment
Brit. Honduras	50	21	28 (4,500 persons)
Fiji	70	35	30 (39,000 „)
Mauritius	95	71	40 (90,000 „)
Swaziland	24	16	22 (11,500 „)
West Indies:			
Barbados	91		20 (31,800 „)
Guiana	33		11 (21,000 „)
Jamaica	23	69	10 (46,500 „)
St. Kitts	92		58 (5,000 „)
Trinidad	5		12 (23,600 „)

Source: the same as for table 14, p. 5.

Clearly, Mauritius is the country most dependent on the guaranteed sales of sugar in the UK; it is no exaggeration to say that its national economy stands and falls with these exports. But even with the other countries listed, the percentages of total exports affected by the possibility of exporting sugar to Britain are considerable.

Now let us assume that, after joining the Common Market, Britain were obliged to take over the EEC's surplus of sugar. For the 1970/71 season this surplus was estimated at 1 million tons. Taking a look at table 14 we will observe that this EEC surplus would take the place of the 150,000 tons Britain imported at world market prices and a further 850,000 tons of the guaranteed CSA sugar.[54] Roughly, this means that the CSA countries would be able to dispose of only half their sugar exports to the UK, provided domestic sugar production in Britain remained at the level indicated in table 14. However, this is an unreasonable supposition, for British sugar producers will be able to realise the same (i.e. higher) prices as producers in the EEC are currently receiving. This will inevitably result in greatly increased sugar production in Britain. For apart from the fact that in the enlarged Community producers will have to be awarded equally, it is not unlikely that British sugar producers will bring pressure to bear on the authorities to raise their production quotas substantially. After all, the farmers on the Continent have production quotas that are far in excess of their home consumption. Are British farmers likely to be content with quotas representing less than half of Britain's consumption, merely to oblige their opposite numbers in the EEC?[55]

174

I do not think one needs to be a pessimist to fear that the sugar producers in the developing countries will be the losers in the struggle for the sugar market which is bound to be waged within the enlarged Community. In fact, the fight has already started, as was apparent during the last but one meeting between Britain and the Six on 16th March last. The real issue, then as on so many occasions, was a difference of opinion between France and the other five concerning the volume of sugar imports to be guaranteed to the CSA countries after the CSA agreement expires in 1974. They all agreed that Australia, not being a developing country, need not be guaranteed anything. But that still leaves some 1.3 m. tons of sugar which does come from developing countries. On 16th March the Five thought that this quantity should be permanently imported into the enlarged Community from these developing countries. France, by mouth of Schumann (now also Chairman of the Council), did not then wish to go beyond 5-600,000 tons. I need hardly say that this is far too little; the quotas of the West Indies and Guiana alone exceed 600,000 tons!

They do not seem to worry about that in France. In the Dutch monthly *Suiker Unie* we read that the French Federation of Beetgrowers has called upon its members to increase production this year to a maximum of 145 per cent of the national quota. One of the motives given for this is that they want to anticipate Britain's entry so as to be in a strong position when the new quotas are allocated. If French beet producers respond to this call – and why should they not? – the EEC's sugar surplus will increase by about 400,000 tons.[56]

At the last round of negotiations between Britain and the Six on 12th and 13th May, the French government appeared to have modified its standpoint. The question of the Commonwealth sugar-producing countries was not to be a stumbling block to British membership, so they announced. At the same time, they refused to commit themselves beyond the vague formula: 'protection of the interests of the Commonwealth Sugar Agreement will be respected'.[57] Although the British government had in the past put up a much more spirited defence of these interests, negotiator Rippon on this occasion resigned himself to this very feeble promise. It is no exaggeration to say that the negotiating parties dealt very recklessly with the interests of the developing countries in question. How, after all, can the latter hope for favourable results if in 1974 the CSA has to be renewed and their sugar exports have to be weighed against the sugar production of the Six, which by then will probably have risen sharply? The change in the French attitude would, therefore, appear to be no more than a tactical move:

175

what was stated in so many words on 16th March, may well be the language of facts in 1974.

Evidently, the enlargement of the European Economic Community has quite a lot in store for the developing countries. In the foregoing I have given only a few instances of what is at stake. It is time we realised that these things are about to happen (in the negotiating chambers and, before long, in the implementation of the policy) without the future victims having any say in the matter. Entirely in keeping with the Centre-Periphery mechanism, their fate is settled behind their backs.

IV. EVALUATION

The conclusions drawn incidentally in the previous chapters do not need to be repeated in full here. The broad lines emerging from our discourses point to the following:

1. The European Community is an important part of the Centre of the world economy, and will be to an even greater extent once the Community is enlarged to ten member states. It is, moreover, an area with a rapidly growing number of special relations with Periphery countries. The policy in regard to these special relations (both the association policy pursued up till now, and the alignment of the Community in regard to the reorganisation of Britain's special relations) appears to be based on a mixture of two notions: (1) the conferment of certain advantages (aid and trade) upon particular less developed developing countries, and (2) the consolidation and enlargement of a European sphere of influence in Africa and the Mediterranean (the inclusion of Israel within this sphere entails the need to establish links with a few other states in the Middle East as well).

2. In the policy the European Community has pursued to date we cannot find a single indication of a political desire to use this important Centre position for the purpose of bringing about a change in the hierarchic international system in the sense of diminishing the contrasts with the lower levels. Any attempts there may be to change this system are aimed merely at restoring Europe to the absolute top level. In that context the relations with developing countries serve only as a means of enhancing Europe's political and economic importance.

3. Initiatives in the field of development aid are taken only: (a) if in some way or other they serve the Community's own interests (e.g.

176

the proposal for the International Oils and Fats Agreement), or (b) if the cost is not too great (e.g. the mutual preferences granted to associated countries), or (c) if such initiatives (e.g. the General Preference System) do not run counter to the Community's own aims (the creation of a European sphere of influence).

4. Co-operation in measures relating to development aid is likewise withheld if Community interests had to be sacrificed (e.g. non-participation in the International Sugar Agreement), or potential benefits were reduced (e.g. the chance that after 1974 Britain will be unable to continue meeting its obligations under the Common-wealth Sugar Agreement).

5. In the drafting and implementation of the Community's policy, the problem of striking a balance between the divergent and frequently conflicting interests of the individual member states is often so complex that any interests of third parties (e.g. developing countries) cannot carry any weight (e.g. the Common Agricultural Policy or the negotiations on enlargement). Consequently, the repercussions this has on the economies of the developing countries are unavoidable; nor is there a competent body that can seriously examine such repercussions and recommend compensatory or redressing measures.

The reader may wonder whether this harsh verdict on the European Community is really called for. After all, Weil says: 'The primary objective of the European Community is not to create some kind of common policy for Europe's relations with the rest of the world. The objective is unity – in the first instance this means economic unity – which implies an essentially inward-looking orientation'. To this one might want to add that neither is the main objective of the Community to aid the underdeveloped peoples of the world in their emancipation and advance towards an existence worthy of human beings. But does that settle the question? Must we accept this reasoning as an excuse in advance for the failure of the Community to aspire to, let us say, a global vision? I don't think so.

There might be some justification for this excuse if we were concerned with an institution which (a) had not been created for this purpose, and (b) had not exercised much influence on it, either. But this is certainly not true of the European Community, as we have seen from the preceding chapters. Like all other prosperous countries, the Community is bang in the middle of the problems of the developing countries. These development problems, as explained in the first chapter, essentially have the character of a Centre-Periphery contradistinction on a global scale. In this situation there can be no excuse for an inward-looking orientation, since it can only aggravate the imbalance of the international system.

There is just one more thing I would mention. In chapters II and III we did not look into the aid activities, except for a single comment on the European Development Fund, not even in those cases where there actually is a Community Policy (as for deliveries of food). I do not believe that the inclusion of these activities in our evaluation would have led to different conclusions (conclusion No. 3, for example, is especially relevant to the aforementioned food aid, because this amounts to an (admittedly sensible) disposal of Europe's wheat and dairy surpluses).

Nor do I believe that it is so very regrettable at this stage that there is yet no Community policy in regard to development aid. I would say that those who consider this desirable do so primarily because they think it is an aim worth pursuing in view of the necessary unification of Europe. What I am afraid of is that integration on this point, like so many of the European activities that have so far been combined, amounts to a grouping together under the smallest common denominator. For instance, there is no reason to expect that a Common Development Policy will in all respects go as far as the Dutch standpoint as it has up till now been officially proclaimed (we will not discuss its implementation here), even though this Dutch standpoint cannot even be called adequate. To my mind, the question whether a common policy on this point is desirable, depends solely on what its substance will be. As long as this cannot reasonably be expected to feature those priorities that make a start with the reversal of the tendencies we have pointed to in the foregoing pages, I think it would be better if the Netherlands remained uncommitted on this issue, and by all possible means, jointly with other industrialised countries that support a truly global vision, threw in the scales its political weight as a 'small' country. This does not rule out seizing every opportunity that presents itself in the Community to raise this vitally important question and to convince the Community partners of its urgency (possibly in the form of a debate on the formulation of a Common Development Policy). The aim, then, should be: the right development policy; not the communal character it may have.

178

NOTES

1. *S. Sideri:* Perspectives for the Third World (in: Internationale Spectator, No. 5, 8 March 1971, p. 472 et seq.).
2. In his thesis Sideri, following Parsons' example, defines power as 'a specific mechanism operating in the process of social interaction to bring about changes in the preference structure of one's own subsystem or other subsystems'. (*S. Sideri:* Trade and Power, UPR, 1970, p. 8). This definition implies the possibility that the process of exercising power (the influencing) is so successful that it meets with no resistance.
3. *O. C. Cox:* Capitalism as a system (Monthly Review Press, New York, 1964, p. 3).
4. In his article in the Internationale Spectator, Sideri criticises the American T. P. Thornton for writing: 'In the short and medium term, our (USA's) interests are frequently parallel to Moscow's, and our conflict over how the world will be organised has more ideological than operational significance'. (T. P. Thornton: A View from Washington, in: Annals of the American Academy of Political and Social Sciences, November 1969).
5. See the address by Emilio Maspero, general secretary of the CLASC in: Towards Internationalised Development Action, Report of the International Working-Congress of Action-Groups on International Development, Egmond-aan-Zee, 1970, p. 60.
6. *J. Galtung:* Political Development and the International Environment, An Essay on Imperialism (unpublished stencil, Vienna, Aug. '70).
7. This picture is, of course, not entirely novel, and has much in common with the Marxist vision on the international class struggle. One point of difference, however, is that in Galtung's model there is definitely a concord of interests as between the centres of the Centre and the Periphery countries, but not between the peripheries of the two groups of countries. For Galtung maintains that the centre-periphery contrast in the Centre countries is smaller than the centre-periphery contrast in the Periphery countries, which is more or less borne out by, inter alia, the statistics on the distribution of incomes in the rich countries compared with that in the developing countries. This means that the periphery groups in the industrialised countries (e.g. the workers) will be more inclined towards a community of interests with their own centre groups (e.g. the entrepreneurs or the government) than with the periphery groups in the developing countries. Global solidarity between all the lower groups in the world is not very likely in this concept.
8. If we break down the group of industrialised countries into capitalist and communist countries, the rise in exports by the developing countries to the former was 81.8 per cent and to the latter 108.3 per cent. Corresponding figures for imports by the developing countries from the two groups: imports from the former increased by 72 per cent, those from the latter by no less than 192 per cent. However, the communist countries' share is still fairly small. (East-West trade, incidentally, advanced by 145 per cent).
9. The terms of trade (export price index divided by import price index) of the developing countries fell by 3.9% in the period from 1960 to 1969. See: UNCTAD, Review of International Trade and Development, 1969/70 (TD/B/309, 7 Aug. '70), p. 38.

10. *Celso Furtado:* Obstacles to Development in Latin America (Anchor Books, New York, 1970), p. 22.
11. This certainly does not apply to all developing countries. Furtado observes that in consequence of the penetration of American conglomerates in such countries as Argentina, Brazil and Mexico, countries that had already passed through the first stages of industrialisation, 'the development of an entrepreneurial class having clear-cut national feelings was interrupted'. 'National entrepreneurial action was restricted to secondary or decadent sectors or to the opening up of new fields, which eventually would be taken over by the large foreign organisations.' See *C. Furtado,* op. cit. p. 35.
12. Handelsblad/NRC, 16 Jan. 1971.
13. *Celso Furtado:* op. cit. p. 55.
14. Handelsblad/NRC, 16 Feb. 1971.
15. *S. Sideri,* op. cit. in Internationale Spectator, p. 490.
16. UNCTAD: Review of Maritime Transport, 1969 (TD/B/C. 4/66), pp. 4 and 8.
17. *N. P. Gleditsch:* Trends in World Airline Patterns (in: Journal of Peace Research, Vol. 4, 1967, p. 366).
18. *S. Sideri,* op. cit. in Internationale Spectator, p. 492.
19. Haan points out that the standpoint of the Group of Ten at the time of the creation of the new Special Drawing Rights did not take into account the typical balance of payments problem of the developing countries. See: *R. L. Haan:* Special Drawing Rights and Development, Leyden 1971, pp. 11 and 65-67.
20. World Bank: Trends in Developing Countries, August 1970.
21. Sideri quotes a number of publications which clearly show the large extent to which the payment balances of the US, the UK, and France benefited from the strings attached to the aid. See: *S. Sideri,* op. cit. in Internationale Spectator, pp. 483-84.
22. It should be noted that, as is customary in trade statistics, the EEC figure consists of the sum of the imports of the six individual EEC nations, and thus includes intra-EEC trade.
23. This latter figure was calculated by reference to data the Dutch Government furnished to the Lower Chamber when the new association agreements were discussed (Session 1969-1970 – 10 606, supplementary memorandum No. 7, appendices A and B). From the same data it is possible to calculate that five AASM countries (Ivory Coast, Niger, Togo, Chad and Congo Braz.) succeeded in doubling their exports to the EEC between 1960 and 67, whereas the combined AASM exports increased by only 56 per cent. (The attentive reader will have noted that in this case the rise in total AASM exports to the EEC is calculated at 56 per cent over the period 1960-67, whereas in an earlier paragraph there is reference to a 54 per cent increase over a longer period, viz. 1960-1968. This does not mean that AASM exports to the EEC declined between 1967 and 68. The difference results from the use of two different sources. Unable to offer an explanation, I merely mention the discrepancy so as to avoid any misunderstanding).
24. The effective tariff is calculated by expressing the difference between the nominal tariffs on two successive processing phases of a product in percentages of the added value obtained by such processing. Hence, the effective tariff is an expression of the duty imposed on processing in the exporting country.

180

25. Cf. the study by Bela Balassa (UNCTAD, TD/69). Since this study was compiled some changes have been made in the CET, but they do not materially affect the essence of Balassa's conclusions.
26. Data derived from: M. Z. Cutajar/A. Franks: The Less Developed Countries in World Trade (London, ODI, 1967).
27. Cf.: Conclusions of a consultation organised by the 'Office Catholique d'Information sur les Problèmes Européens' (OCIPE), Dec. 3-5, 1970, Brussels.
28. 'De EEG landbouw in internationaal verband' (EEC agriculture in an international context) is the title of a report by Mrs. M. J. 't Hooft-Welvaars to the Nederlandse Vereniging voor Staathuishoudkunde; see the bound reports in: Het EEG Landbouwbeleid (EEC Agricultural policy), The Hague, 1970.
29. Cf.: Changes in EEC imports of commodities affected by the variable levy system (ERS-Foreign 225, US Department of Agriculture, Washington, June 1968), p. 5.
30. SER-ISEA: Recommendations concerning the European Commission's statement to the Council regarding directives for an international agreement on oils and fats (Jan. 1970).
31. See the aforementioned report by Mrs. 't Hooft-Welvaars, p. 76.
32. The SER report deals with the European Commission's idea of stabilising world market prices of oils and fats and ensuring increasing revenue for the developing countries by means of an International Agreement on Oils and Fats. According to the Commission, such an Agreement would have to consist of a stabilisation levy on imports into the industrialised countries, which would then have to be used for paying compensation to the exporting developing countries and for financing buffer stocks and food aid. The report arrives at the conclusion that such a stabilisation levy is more likely to have a destabilising effect, and suspects that the real purpose of the Commission's proposal was merely to ensure stabilisation of *EEC import prices* at a certain, relatively high level, in order to lend support to the European agricultural policy. Mrs. 't Hooft-Welvaars' main objection to these proposals of the Commission is 'that symptoms (low prices) are fought, instead of causes (extra-marginal production). If the intention is really to help the developing countries by improving world market prices of oils and fats, the remedy is to curb production in those areas where diversification into entirely different industries is easiest: in the industrialised countries'. (p. 33).
33. Monthly Journal of the Netherl. Sugar Union, No. 9, Sept. 1970, p. 171.
34. Mrs. 't Hooft-Welvaars' report, p. 26.
35. Another adverse factor has been exports to the free markets of the world by Eastern bloc countries not affiliated to the ISA of Cuban sugar reaching them via the Soviet Union (which *is* a member of the ISA).
36. On the other hand, since 1st Jan. of this year a few Orders have become operative which facilitate the importation of several CAP products from the AASM/DOM/TOM.
37. This trend was not noted by the Dutch ministers who signed the above-mentioned Parliamentary Paper. They did state that they deemed it desirable 'that Dutch industry should have more scope to develop in these countries'.
38. *G. L. Weil:* A Foreign Policy for Europe? p. 137. According to Weil French influence is also responsible for the fact that the EDF has up till now been

reluctant to co-operate with other aid agencies, such as those of the UN (see p. 160).

39. *Stuart de la Mahotiere:* Towards One Europe (p. 240), quoted by *E. Pearse and R. Kahn,* The White Tribes of Europe (p. 11).

40. *G. L. Weil:* op. cit., p. 171.

41. European Parliament, Records of the 1970-71 session, Document No. 167, 16 November 1970.

42. Weil suggests that the initiative for this agreement came from the Commission, so that it might serve as '. . . a kind of diplomatic smokescreen to detract from the prominence that would have been given to the Israeli agreement as the first that the Community has concluded'. See *G. L. Weil,* op cit., p. 190.

43. See *G. L. Weil,* op cit. p. 192.

44. I mention only the appeal the Italian M. P. Giuseppe Vedovato addressed to his fellow parliamentarians in the member states of the Council of Europe in: 'Europe and the Developing World: a call for action', Strassbourg, 1 Dec. 1970.

45. The development aid activities of the various member states' governments are, of course, often directed at other developing countries as well, but apart from the general observations in chapter I, I shall not deal with them within the scope of this study.

46. See Explanatory Memorandum to the Bill giving approval to the Yaoundé association agreement, Parliamentary Paper 10 606, 1969/70, No. 3, p. 5.

47. For certain 'sensitive' products such as textile and mineral oil products there are divergent rules. In several cases the buffer clause is less than 50 per cent, and the supplementary quota is fixed at a lower percentage or is dropped altogether.

48. As a result of faulty reports in many newspapers, a great deal of misunderstanding has arisen on this point. Several comments proceeded from the assumption that textiles and footwear had been excluded from the entire GPS, which is not so. The fact that the dependent countries have been excluded in respect of these products is connected with their links with other industrialised countries, and – as in Hong Kong's case – with their strong competitive position as regards these sensitive products.

49. For most of the data in this paragraph the author has drawn on: *M. Z. Cutajar & A. Franks,* The Less Developed Countries in World Trade (1967).

50. See M. Z. Cutajar & A. Franks, op. cit., p. 91. The preferential margin is the difference between the normal and the preferential tariff on a product. The abovementioned average preferential margin has been found by taking the average margins by category of goods and weighing them with the import value of each category.

51. See Parliamentary Report 10 606, No. 3, p. 5.

52. *M. Subhan:* Commonwealth's Last Chance (in: Far Eastern Economic Review, No. 25, 18 June 1970, p. 47).

53. The two previous sentences are deliberately in the past tense, because the differences on this point between Britain and the EEC are already vanishing, more or less in anticipation of Britain's entry. The British government is changing its agricultural policy in such a way that domestic producers will be able to supply a larger proportion of the home market; more import levies will be introduced in order to protect this market, whilst the agricultural subsidies will gradually be switched from the exchequer to the consumer.

54. In the Annual Report of the LEI (Netherl. Agric. Econ. Institute), Maris presents an entirely different, and to my mind, very misleading calculation. He puts Britain's sugar imports in 1968 at 2.04 m. tons (OECD data), and the EEC surplus at only 150,000 tons (an incomprehensibly low figure; Maris probably dit not include French DOM sugar, but even if that is omitted, which is wrong, for the DOM is considered part of the EEC, the EEC surplus would still be of the order of magnitude of 400,000 tons). On the basis of these figures, with the EEC surplus accounting for only 8 per cent of total British imports of sugar, Maris arrives at the conclusion that this 'will have a limited influence on the developing countries' sugar exports'. (See: Annual Report 1969, Agricultural Economic Institute, The Hague, p. 36).
55. Here it should be pointed out that the current Danish award to sugar producers is even lower than in Britain, and that an adjustment of the prices in that country will doubtless lead to even greater increases in production.
56. Maandblad Suiker Unie, No. 3, March 1971, p. 46.
57. Handelsblad/NRC, 13th May 1971.

Summary of the discussions

J. P. Pronk: 'I would like to underline the necessity, which Cohen seems to deny, of using an analytical model in order to understand the particular problems we are dealing with. Cohen did not start from an explicit model, but if we look at his paper, it seems that implicitly he does use one, which is: the central question is the regulation of economic relations between states (see p. 109). I think this model is confusing, because it suggests that a completely new situation arose after the Treaty of Rome and after the developing countries became independent toward the end of the 'fifties and began to formulate their demands. This would mean that there was a break between the 'fifties and 'sixties, a vacuum which had to be filled. In my opinion, the development policies of the Six are a necessary consequence, a complement to policies followed in the past. There is continuity, and in the light of the foreign policy goals of the nations concerned this policy has rightly been called neocolonialistic. And to a large extent it still is. There is no gap, but traits which are permanent over time.

Coppens has made an effort to explain these tendencies and he uses a model, with which, contrary to what you would expect, I do not agree. He uses the centre-periphery model, which has been used and developed by others like Prebisch, Bettelheim and Frank before. They all use this type of model, distinguishing it from the Tinbergen-type poor-rich model, because they concentrate on a specific kind of relationship. The rich are rich, not because they are rich, but because they keep the poor poor. The neocolonialist-imperialist relationship is inherent and essential in the models of these authors. Now, while Coppens uses this model, he confuses the issues, because however deplorable the policies of the EEC are – which he shows – he fails to show that the Six have been able to sustain their growth and wealth *because* of this policy of exploitation of the Third World. This has not been proved by him, nor by anyone else in the literature on development problems. Therefore, we cannot yet use this model, because it has not empirically been proved correct.

This confusion is dangerous, because it has consequences for the policy conclusions, as well as for the analysis itself. What Coppens does is in fact to sketch a relationship, as Tinbergen does, which is a negation relationship. The EEC, the USA and Eastern Europe built up their systems and blocs, neglecting the Third World and the deplorable effect their policies have on the Third World. But this negation is not inherent and essential for their own growth potential.

Although I am still not convinced by the empirical testing of the centre-periphery model, I feel constrained to use the negation and the neocolonialist model, which are complementary to one another. But one cannot say that the policy of the rich must *of necessity* be as it is because they would put their economic wellbeing at stake if they behaved differently. This implies that there are possibilities of changes, which would not endanger or frustrate the future of the economic powers concerned. I accept Coppens' analysis of the past policies of the EEC and share his conclusions. But I disagree on the point of the policy implications. I see a possibility of bridging the seemingly large gap between Coppens and Cohen (which would not be possible if one were to argue from a purely neomarxist model). They are not diametrically opposed, but rather complementary, and their analyses can lead to policies that can be implemented within the framework of a harmonymodel and international co-operation.'

Various other speakers raised a number of points concerning the centre-periphery model, its application to the policies of the European Community and the policy implications to be drawn from the analysis.

A. Mozer: 'The last words of Coppens, when he stated his belief in policies carried out by the individual states, give evidence of enormous political naivety. It consists in believing that the policies of the member countries would not be equally bad if there were no common development policy of the Community. I agree with his analysis of the depressing record of the EEC in respect of the development problem. It is very doubtful, however, whether the development policy of, for instance, the Netherlands would be much better if they were not tied to the Community. In all my years in Brussels I have never seen any minister or government who behaved better than the others. It is in the politics at home, that a start should be made.

It is naive to think that obstruction of the Community's policy per se will lead to better development policies.'

H. C. Posthumus Meyjes: 'One of the central questions to me seems to be: how are European co-operation and integration related to the problems of development? Is integration by definition disadvantageous for the Third World e.g. because of self-sufficiency and international division of labour? Coppens' use of the centre-periphery model is interesting, but it becomes less interesting in the course of his paper. He uses it only as a description of the situation, which is no more than interesting. But it does not lead to specific conclusions and recommendations, based on the model. The question really is, whether the exist-

188

ence of the EEC does in fact reinforce the system, as described, and make it worse. This is not shown by Coppens. And indeed it seems a difficult thing to do in general. In some ways it did make things worse, in others it improved the situation (e.g. in helping to bring about a system of general preferences). In his conclusions he stresses the point that the EEC had no development policy. This is not strange, since the development of the Third World was not one of the goals of the Community and indeed the possibilities and power of the Community per se remain limited. On the other hand, he clearly contradicts himself in saying that it was a good thing that the EEC had no policy, because that would have made things worse.'

H. A. J. Coppens: 'I agree, that the way I used the centre-periphery model is different from its use by some of the authors cited, like Frank and Bettelheim. It may not be useful to prove the existence of relations of exploitation but it is useful to refine the negation-model, as used by Tinbergen, because it adds to the realisation that the poor are becoming more and more dependent upon the rich, while the rich are becoming less and less dependent upon the poor. The relations of dependency are thus better taken care of than in the simple poor-rich model. In addition, the centre-periphery model not only looks at the relations between states, but also within states, and shows that the contradictions between states can be explained from the harmony between the centre countries and the centre groups in the periphery countries.

I have deliberately concentrated only on an adequate description of the relations between the EEC countries and the Third World, because this is a pre-condition for any policy recommendations. But these do come later.'

POLICY IMPLICATIONS

J. P. Pronk: 'The policy conclusions centre around the question whether we should continue to work for a common development policy, on the course set in 1957. Many people support this course, especially in the European Parliament, where the criticism is not very serious. In general these critics do accept the thesis that those things which can be done collectively should not be done separately, no matter what the content of such a common policy would be. In recent discussions the European Parliament has rejoiced over the fact that the EEC conforms to goals set for the Second Development Decade, but if one looks closer this appears to apply to the goals set by the Pearson

189

Report, which is a list of goals set by the rich and in which the poor had no say. These discussions overlook the central question, which is what the goals of a real development policy should be. And this also seems to be the case in Cohen's paper, as he discusses the future of the common development policy. As I said, the central question is whether the now existing common policy, carried out by the member states is really a step ahead compared with what would be the case if all carried out their policies independently. Another, related, question is whether this common policy has had a positive or negative influence on the possibilities of working toward decisionmaking on problems of international trade and aid in a really supra-national framework where not some but all developing countries have an equal say with the rich countries.

With regard to the first question I really do have the impression that the common development policy has not been a step forward. Aid has not increased, and the funds of the European development programme go to a limited number of African countries, as would have been the case under bilateral (French) programmes. Measures reached in other fields, such as the trade policy are indeed more positive and (small) steps in the right direction. But they were taken only after a number of steps backwards, through the protectionist policy of self-sufficiency and through discrimination in the provision of aid to certain countries and not to others, and in the tariff policies. On balance the result is not positive.

We see evidence in the EEC of the fear, shown for instance by Galtung, that the formation of blocs is not helpful for the solution of fundamental problems. The larger and the more powerful the blocs become, the more remote becomes the possibility of an international decisionmaking process, which is able to reach just solutions, because all nations are represented. This does not apply to the EEC only, but also to the US and the Eastern bloc. They reduce the possibilities of dealing with fundamental worldwide problems in a truly international setting, such as the UN and its organs, the IMF, the World Bank and UNCTAD.

But indeed, in many respects there is no way back from the common EEC politics in the fields relating to development of the Third World. It would be futile to argue that there is such a way.

Yet, other conclusions may also be drawn:
1. No new functions and tasks in the field of development should be given to the Community, for instance in the field of the international monetary aspects of the development problem, or in the

field of a possible future common foreign policy. We can also think of the area of private investments and production policies. It is not certain that these national policies would be better than a common EEC policy, but at least the formation of a new centre of power, which would inhibit in advance a real multilateral attack on these problems, is prevented.

2. In those fields where there is no way back, efforts should concentrate on making the policies as open as possible. The least developed countries should be favored.

3. In countries like the Netherlands there are opportunities to pursue new policies, through a change in public opinion. I may be mistaken in the behaviour of our Ministers in Brussels, as Mozer pointed out. But he seems to underestimate the changes in public opinion and their impact: We should:

   a. go ahead, where possible together with others such as the Scandinavian countries, to promote complementary policies within the international framework of the UN;

   b. where we find that the EEC is too narrow-minded and unconstructive, try to find compensation for the negative effects of such policies, in sofar as they are our responsibility, for instance by way of additional aid as a compensation for negative trade policies or, by providing extra resources to countries like Turkey, help to offset and solve the problem of foreign migratory labour;

   c. in the field of production policies – where there is scope for manoeuvre – pay more attention to the vital need for a restructuring of the international division of labour.

Finally, it seems necessary to transfer our freedom of movement and decisionmaking as much as possible to those organs which are really multilateral.

We can anticipate the formation of worldwide centres of decisionmaking through these transfers. The vicious circle of powerlessness can be broken in this way. Our freedom of movement is greater than is often suspected. This freedom should be used. A development policy has many complementary components. And we can, through our anticipatory moves, promote a more fundamental change in the world structure, in order to realise the goals set by the developing countries themselves. These are not merely economic growth, as seems to be emphasized here (as is so often the case). These goals are much more defined by the principle of self-reliance: the possibility of determining for oneself one's economic, political and cultural goals. And we can help to offset, through compensatory measures, the negative influences which the rich countries have on this possibility of self-reliance.'

H. A. J. Coppens: 'I would like to agree with those who say that in many respects there is no way back and that there is no guarantee that independent policies would be better. But I would not want to lose the possibilities which lie in some parts of the official development policy of the Netherlands and which seem to be backed by public opinion. At present a common development policy would not go nearly as far, as is evident if one looks at France and Germany. Therefore, we should try to retain as much power as possible in our own hands.

I have not fully discussed in my paper the question, raised by several people, whether the problems of the developing countries have become worse just because of the integration process of the EEC, nor whether indeed individual policies of the Six would have been more positive.

It is difficult to show that the process of integration in itself has reinforced the hierarchical international system, but I have shown a number of negative consequences of the integration process such as, for instance, the common agricultural policy. Perhaps it would have been unrealistic to accuse the EEC of having too little concern for the Third World, if only the effects had been neutral. But I have indeed tried to show that the EEC policies have had some harmful effects for the developing countries, and the inwardlooking orientation is responsible for the fact that nothing has been done to compensate these effects. The EEC was not neutral at all, by letting the model work as it does. I have indeed not given detailed guidelines for an alternative policy. The first step was to see what really happens. This analysis should lead to policy recommendations. Pronk has outlined a number of them, to which I agree, and we should try to convince our political parties of the necessity of them. I would like to add that we should not only not transfer a number of tasks to the EEC but we should also make our willingness to come to common European policies conditional upon the attitudes of our European partners toward more worldwide arrangements. So in addition to retaining a number of tasks in national hands, we can in some respects slow down the process of European integration in order to strengthen worldwide interests. Although the outline of an alternative policy is still vague, it should certainly reflect the notion that all our policies within the EEC should be judged against their impact on the interests of the developing countries and the world at large.'

J. C. P. A. van Esch: 'All too often, it seems to me, the negative feed-

192

back of development policies on the periphery in the centre-countries is overlooked. The changes which are being advocated – and which are necessary indeed – are clearly at the expense of some people in our societies and usually they are the economically weak and vulnerable. The model used should take this impact into account and should clearly state these consequences, which should then be discussed with the group concerned in order to create a political willingness to accept these policies.

In the second place, I find it difficult to imagine that the freedom of movement will indeed be as large as suggested. There is no question of freedom in the trade policies, and when the common economic and monetary policy is implemented, around 1980 or perhaps 1990, technical and financial aid will be controlled, because it affects the balance of payments, which will be controlled by the Community. I am not optimistic about the possibility of independent policies in this respect.'

R. Cohen: 'Although van Esch seems to overestimate the impact of the common economic and monetary policy – when it comes – and I would be less extreme in my judgment, I would stress that the mere fact, that the EEC is progressing, and integration is becoming more complete, supports the contention that this should imply a common development policy as a necessary complement of what happens in so many other fields, which all have implications for the Third World.

I must say that the opponents of such a common policy are still very vague. Is "a worldwide policy" more than a slogan? What would happen in concrete terms, within the IMF and other organizations, except for the system of general preferences (which still has to be implemented by the respective blocs and states)? I am uncertain about this, unless the aim is a "change of the system", assuming that this is a precondition for the development of the underdeveloped world. But then we are far away in the area of philosophizing about "the just society". We should not forget that in the international field today the EEC is the only kind of organization which is able to take decisions, and through it some others have also been brought to decisions and have been forced to act, which was certainly in the interest of the developing countries.'

LIBERALISATION OF TRADE AND ASSOCIATION POLICIES

J. J. van Geet: 'We seem to assume that trade policy is the central element in the development strategy and that general liberalisation of trade is a thing to work for. But what does one want to realise? On the basis of the model used by Coppens, it seems certain that in the case of liberalisation of trade the most developed among the developing countries would profit most: countries like Mexico, Taiwan and Iran. On the other hand, we seem – taking into account the advantageous position which the industrialised countries already have – to be building a dam against a non-existent flood of competing products from the developing countries.'

H. J. Posthumus Meyjes: 'One of the problems confronting us is the increase in the number of associated countries. One can ask what use there is for such a system of associations, based on the principle of discrimination, if the number becomes so large. What will be the importance of the reversed preferences? Changes will certainly be necessary.'

H. A. J. Coppens: 'It seems necessary indeed to maintain some form of positive discrimination between the more developed and the least developed countries. Otherwise only the relatively industrialised countries would profit from liberalisation. But should such positive discrimination be organized through regional and vertical arrangements? Considering the reinforcement of the centre-periphery system through the strengthening of blocs and regional arrangements, I am very doubtful about this and would in principle prefer universal arrangements. Of course it will be a disadvantage for those countries, which today are associated with the EEC, when they will have to replace this system through the system of general preferences as is now in preparation. But this system reckons with the existence and maintenance of regional arrangements. Compensations could very well be found if we moved toward a real worldwide system, differentiating between the various levels of economic development of the beneficiaries.'

R. Cohen: 'Contrary to what many seem to believe, the goal of a development policy should not be complete liberalisation of trade. Only a limited number of countries would profit from such measures. That is why I am in favour of associations and preferential trade agreements, as long as the picture of an underdeveloped world of identical nations is wrong. It may be true in some fields, but not in many others. As long as this is so, complete liberalisation – which we are not going to have for a long time to come – is dangerous.'

194

J. Kaufmann: 'One element lacking in the analysis presented to us is the need for a structural policy. The relations between Europe, the US, Japan, the Eastern European countries and the Developing countries can no longer be structured rationally by separate individual policies. The problem should be tackled by the EEC, together with the other industrialised countries collectively. Discussions on an international division of labour are necessary. Where and how? Certainly in the suitable UN organs. OECD can also play a useful preparatory role as it did with the general preference system. Again, it is illusory to think that one can solve these problems independently and it is essential that employers and trade unions be brought into the discussion, for the problem cannot be solved without their co-operation.'

H. A. J. Coppens: 'Indeed, liberalisation of trade can bring no solution, because the trade policy deals only with a symptom, caused by differences in production structure, productivity and comparative costs. A way out can only be found in a better and more rational structure of production. The abolition of trade restrictions in itself cannot bring the solution. But these problems, which should be discussed in a worldwide framework, have until now hardly been discussed. And this is true not only of the European Community but of others as well.'

R. Cohen: 'I have been attacked from several sides for having said that justice without order is not possible, and for maintaining that the European Community is contributing to world order and hence to justice. Order and justice cannot be juxtaposed. When chaos reigns no justice is possible and order, at least in principle, offers more possibilities to further justice. The Community offers the advantages that in many difficult negotiations the number of partners is reduced, which increases the chances of agreement. The growing power of the EEC can also become so strong as to force the USA to accept certain changes. The position of the US will remain very strong, but the tighter the unity of the Community, the more pressure can be exerted on the US, which will favor the position of the developing countries.'

FRANCE, THE COMMUNITY AND THE ASSOCIATED AFRICAN STATES

The position of France was brought up from several sides. Was it not true that France, under the cloak of 'development' and the flag of the EEC, was in fact pursuing a policy in Africa, aimed at the maintenance

195

of a power-political bloc, which implies the undoing of universal arrangements, as laid down in the IMF and GATT? This policy had already been apparent at the first UNCTAD conference. The development policy of the Community, it was said, served first of all these French interests and not those of the African countries. A solution would be not to extend the common development program, but to work for more truly multilateral arrangements.

T. W. Crul: 'One of the French conditions for the EEC was the creation of a fund through which France could maintain and finance its overseas interests. And France was successful in this design. For years the African countries had sent their development programs and requests first to Paris, where they were checked against the French plans, after which they were sent back with amendments, before they finally arrived in Brussels.'

H. H. Maas: 'If this is true, it has been accepted with open eyes by the others. It was already in the Schuman Declaration and in the resolutions of the Messina conference. It should be noted for the sake of historical accuracy, that this has always been the French policy and it has not been resisted by the others.'

R. Cohen: 'I find it difficult to make this distinction between French power policy and development. Surely the developing countries in Africa have profited from the Development Program and the system of association with the preferences, contained in it.'

P. J. Kapteyn: 'But French policy has been pure imperialism. It has nothing to do with power politics, anti-Americanism or anti-universalism. Its goal was to safeguard the markets for French industry, and the aid to Africa was essentially aid to French industry.'

Summary and conclusions

H. H. MAAS

It is not an easy task to give a summary and evaluation of the conference papers and the contributions to the discussions, which are reproduced on the preceding pages. Let us begin with looking again at the questions we asked ourselves at the beginning of this conference and see whether answers and, if so, what answers were given to these questions.

The first question was whether co-operation and integration in the framework of an enlarged European Economic Community will be beneficial or detrimental or perhaps neutral or indifferent to the development of harmonious and peaceful relations between Western and Eastern Europe. In the second place, we asked the question whether such an enlarged Community will probably contribute to the solution of the economic and social problems of the Third World, or whether it might have a negative effect on the solution of these same problems.

The political aspects in a stricter sense as well as the military-strategic aspects of the East-West relations in Europe were deliberately kept out of the discussion or were only marginally discussed, because they really need separate treatment. Thus the impact of the enlargement on the German question – which is now at least in the state of movement – was only occasionally touched upon.

Also, in order not to extend our subject matter beyond manageable proportions, it was decided to leave aside for the moment the relations between the enlarged Community and the United States. We realised, however, that this is a debatable point, especially with regard to the problems of development policy, which cannot really be tackled without taking into account the necessity of reaching a consensus on this policy with the other industrialised countries, such as the US and Japan.

The various papers are all based on the realistic assumption that the United Kingdom and at least two of the other candidate-members will indeed join the EEC at that time (in the case of Norway there is more reason to challenge the assumption; at least a number of serious problems have to be solved in this respect).

When the enlargement becomes reality, it is to be expected that it will be possible for a number of developing countries, which now have special relations with the United Kingdom, to convert this special relationship into some form of association with the EEC. Contrary to what is suggested by Coppens (p. 170) this will also include the Asian states in question.

The structure of world trade will undergo profound changes as a consequence of the extension of the Common Market. This conference was, at least in part, motivated by the concern that the external effects of this extension are often more or less taken for granted and anyway much less discussed than the effects on the institutions and functioning of the Community itself. This fact implicitly might reflect a too narrow 'Euro-centric' vision.

It is safe to say that the enlargement of the EEC will have lasting and strong effects on the system of international relations in general. But it is far more difficult to go beyond the enumeration of trends and possibilities. One of the areas in which these effects will be felt is in the formation of blocs and alignments within the United Nations and the specialized organizations, such as GATT and IMF in particular. These effects will increase as co-operation and integration in the Community deepen.

The first part of the conference and hence of this book deals with the consequences of the enlargement of the EEC for the relations between Western Europe on the one hand, and the socialist countries, organized in the Comecon, and the European neutrals, on the other.

The most visible consequence will be a loss of function for the EFTA. It will no longer be able to play its present, albeit limited, role. Some of the member states will become members of the EEC, others will remain outside. What will happen to them?

Some cases were discussed in more detail, others, like Portugal were not mentioned at all. It seems clear, however, that the problems of these countries need to be taken seriously. Assuming that membership is excluded as a possibility (for various reasons), association also raises a number of problems, as does the suggestion of preferential trade agreements. The most acceptable solution seems to lie – as Dahrendorff has suggested – in some form of general lowering of tariffs, in order to find compensation for those industrialised states which will remain outside the Community. This might be feasible, especially for industrial products. On the other hand, some kind of free trade structure, like the one now existing among the EFTA countries, and consisting of the remaining countries and the enlarged Community could be considered. The former construction is much more attractive than the latter, because the connection of the Common Market with other industrialised countries in the form of a free trade agreement – although theoretically possible – would raise such serious technical problems that an early solution could not be expected.

As said before, the purely political and security aspects of the East-West relations were not the subject of the various contributions to the conference and to this volume. It was only occasionally observed that the extension of the EEC will doubtlessly have serious political consequences, although this will not necessarily lead to more political unity. Pinder argued that the enlarged Community would tend to become more like the Swiss and less like the Prussian model of federation. However, one can only hope that this will indeed be the case. The question whether the enlargement of the EEC will result in a re-inforcement or weakening of the Atlantic Community is an equally open question.

In the discussions the question was raised and not fully dealt with, whether the entry of Great Britain would facilitate or lead to a combined Anglo-French nuclear force (to which one could add the possibility of a German contribution in the form of capital and technology). The possibility of such a Western European nuclear force will not be realised overnight, but it remains a serious problem. Much will depend in this respect on the attitude which the Soviet Union will adopt towards the enlarged community. This again is connected with a number of other international questions, such as the relations between the Soviet Union and China on the one hand, and the extent and speed of a 'normalisation' of the relations between China and the United States. An analysis of the potentialities of these developments would carry us far beyond the scope of the present book.

As to the role of the European neutrals with respect to a further *détente* and *rapprochement* between Eastern and Western Europe, Mozer's analysis makes it clear that not much is to be expected from such a role. Pinder in his contribution gives a very interesting analysis of the possibilities in the economic field to foster East-West relations, and he suggested a number of ways in which economic interaction between East and West could be increased. Up till now, the Community has limited itself to a passive role; though in name a form of common policy, the common liberalisation lists were nothing more than an addition of national decisions. The special position of the Soviet Union with respect to this liberalisation was only due to German pressure, and it was eliminated immediately after the conclusions of the Moscow treaty in autumn 1970, without any request for concessions in exchange. Pinder's recommendations for an active common policy are very valuable indeed. Within the EEC there is a growing conviction that a common policy towards the Comecon countries is a necessity, not only from an economic point of view, but also in a legal sense. Recent rulings of the European Court have left little doubt that the authority of member states independently and individually to regulate relations with third countries in the sphere of matters which have become part of the common policy within the Community will be very limited if not non-existent in the near future.

Although their papers do not clearly concur on this point, it seems that both Mozer and Pinder agree that it would be politically dangerous if the Community were to try to sow discord between the Comecon countries. The best it can do is to react as quickly and positively as possible to any divergence which might develop in the economic systems of the Comecon members.

Kaufmann, in his discussion of the institutionalisation of East-West relations, makes it clear how useful and necessary the co-operation within the Economic Commission for Europe is and can be. He stresses the necessity of working through this organization and the fact that there is no need for some new organization.

He raised yet another very interesting point which provided a link between the two themes of our deliberations. Increased economic interaction and trade between East and West will probably first develop in those fields that are also of interest to 'the South'. Consequently, an increase in East and West trade might be detrimental to the interest of the developing countries.

The second topic of discussion: what will be the external effect of the enlargement of the European Community and what will be its role in the world?, is far more difficult to summarize and evaluate. Again we would like to repeat the central question:

To what extent is the extension of the Community favourable or unfavourable for the economic development of the countries of the Third World? Obviously, a discussion on this point cannot escape an evaluation of the implicit or explicit role and policies of the EEC in this respect in the past twelve years. Much criticism has been levied against these policies. Some good things have also been said about them. It is not very useful to repeat these points here. One neglected element, however, needs to be stressed: co-operation of industrialised countries within a common market can and should add to the possibilities of revision and improvement of the international division of labour, and hence of the structures of production in Europe. We should not underestimate the potential of a larger market to absorb the shocks which necessarily will accompany and result from such changes in the inter-

202

national structures of production. It would be very difficult for a country like the Netherlands independently to take decisions which run directly counter to the interests of specific branches of industry, and to sacrifice these interests. But such decisions could more readily be made acceptable in the situation of a large common market, providing new possibilities of expansion in exchange. The importance of this element should not be overlooked.

With regard to the enlargement of the EEC the question arises what will be the effects of this extension on the developing countries. The special relations which a number of countries have had until now with the United Kingdom, will partly be transformed into patterns of association with the Community. We shall have to wait and see what will be the benefits of this pattern of association, but potentially at least it seems to offer chances for increased international trade and a reduction of the discriminating treatment between the various groups of states. For the ones remaining outside the extension it will hardly be profitable. For them, however, the general system of preferential tariffs retains its importance, even in a larger Common Market.

A much bigger stumbling bloc is the common agricultural policy. Coppens has struck a number of dark notes on this score. Too dark sometimes, it seems.

There are two reasons for this:

The first has to do with the fact that, as the figures which Coppens produces, show, the Community is in some respects becoming less self-sufficient. He argues that this would lead the Community to be less serious in its efforts to restrict production. But it can also be argued that it is politically easier to restrict production under these circumstances. In this respect it is not without importance to note – in connection with the production of sugar – that the countries of the Common Market – and this obligation will also apply to England – have undertaken not to increase their area of production. In general, the dangers of increased agricultural production in the UK seem to be overestimated. Secondly, it appears that because of the intra-European relations, the enlarged EEC offers more chances for a lowering of tariffs than the EEC offers at present, which would not be without interest to the developing countries.

Much of the discussion concentrated on the question whether one should be in favour of a common development policy of the EEC or not. However, it was not made clear whether and how the extension would affect the answers to this question. The general consensus seems

203

to be that such a common policy would only be acceptable in sofar as it would mean an improvement of the present situation for the developing countries. But it was doubted whether this was a realistic expectation, and therefore more than one debater demanded that no new tasks and authority in this field should be transferred to the Community. It should be stressed, however, that it may not be so easy to implement such a policy. In the first place it is difficult to calculate whether the result of such a common policy would indeed be worse or better than the result of national actions. But if one accepts the theory – and Cohen has hinted at this mechanism – that there is an immanent tendency in the direction of extension and deepening of areas of co-operation, which lead to an increase in the influence of the Community on the economic policies of the member states, then, when all is said and done, not very much room will remain for independent action. That will certainly not be the case in the area of production policies, and these play a vital role in this connection.

Secondly, it will be difficult to apply this requirement in the field of financial aid, if only because the enlarged EEC will be confronted immediately with the problem of eliminating in one way or another the reversed preferences, which will certainly be compensated partly in the area of financial aid.

The course which the Community will take in the matter of development policies will to a large extent depend upon the development of the political will to do those things which are necessary for a farsighted policy, one which takes the interests of the developing countries as much into account as those of the member states. The political will is one thing, but decisive will be the extent to which this will can be converted into political power. This will have to take place primarily within each country and within the national, political parties, but also on the Community level and in the party formation of that level. Thus the development problem is another reason to tackle the urgent problem of creating a credible counterweight to the European bureaucracy.

Finally, the problem of the relations between the enlarged EEC and the Third World comes down to the question how the world should be organized in order to deal with its most pressing problems, of which the development problem is one. How can the systems of the Six or the Ten be integrated in structures of a worldwide nature, through which a policy of solidarity can be implemented?

It should be stressed here – although this may sound aprioristic – that the economic questions are so much interconnected, that they cannot easily, if at all, be divided into small bits, but should be dealt with in one overall approach. This is one side of the problem. On the other hand, it also seems true that an efficient organization can only come about if the number of participants in decisionmaking, which are also the ones which will have to implement the decisions, remains limited. It seems impossible really to come to grips with the problems in an organization in which each country takes part independently and with equal influence on the decisionmaking, without fully taking into account the prevailing interests and power structure. But again, this question really falls outside the scope of the conference which is reported in this book.